WRITE YOUR OWN WILL

In the same series:
What to Watch Out for When Buying or Selling a House

WRITE YOUR
OWN WILL

by

KEITH BEST, T.D., M.A. (Oxon)

PAPERFRONTS

CONTENTS

DEDICATION
TO MY PARENTS

INTRODUCTION

How to use this book

Chapters 1 to 7 of the book are of general application, and should be studied carefully by all readers. *Chapter 7* largely consists of sample Wills, and one of these, perhaps with slight variations, is likely to suit your purpose.

The later Chapters are important reading for those who are in certain specific circumstances.

Chapter 8 explains what happens if you make no Will at all.

Chapter 9 explains how to make a Will in contemplation of marriage, and is important because otherwise marriage (in England and Wales) automatically revokes a Will previously made.

Chapter 10 shows how it is possible for the courts to disrupt your intention to dispose of your property entirely as you please, because certain people have a legal right to apply to be provided for from your estate. So read Chapter 10 if you intend to try and cut somebody out of your Will!

Chapter 11 shows the powers of the courts to disallow certain bequests because of *conditions* attached by the testator.

Chapter 12 gives a brief resumé of the Inheritance Tax situation, and should be studied by those of substantial means (e.g. House owners).

Chapter 13 explains how the law differs in Scotland.

Chapter 14 explains the different rules which apply to servicemen on active duty.

Chapter 15 explains the procedure your Executors will have to follow in order to obtain probate in England and Wales, which is necessary before they have the legal authority to deal with your Estate.

Lastly, let it be said that a book of this size cannot possibly be a comprehensive guide to every aspect of Will law. A book which was would be a heavy tome running to many hundreds of pages.

The purpose of this book is to help Mr., Mrs. or Miss Average, who has perhaps, at most, say a modest house, a car, and a few thousand pounds to dispose of straightforwardly.

If this is you, then the book is all you need to make a proper legal Will.

However, if you come within the range affected by Inheritance Tax and require tax planning, or if you want to set up complex trusts to benefit either your family or charitable purposes, or if your affairs are in any way complicated, then you should regard this book as being only an introduction to the subject, and seek proper legal advice by consulting your Solicitor.

It is important to understand that the legal position can and does change, so for any but simple Wills legal advice is essential. One of the advantages of this book could be to alert readers to various matters they may not have considered.

Family changes such as deaths, marriages, divorces, illnesses, births etc., often require a new Will to be made at once to bring the position up-to-date.

1

WHO CAN MAKE A WILL?

Virtually anybody who has possessions to dispose of can make a Will. The aim of this simple book is to show you how to do it, and what tax and other considerations should be taken into account.

Everything described in this book you can do yourself; there is no need to go to a lawyer, unless your affairs are particularly complicated or you are very rich. More and more people are making a do-it-yourself Will; in fact about one third of all Wills are now made by people without going to a lawyer, whereas a few years ago it was only one in five. Very few of these Wills fail to take effect because there is something wrong with them.

Subject to matters of tax, which are changing constantly, and to the court's power to intervene in Wills, which is discussed in Chapters 10 and 11, the whole basis of our law on Wills is that anyone should have an unfettered right to dispose of his own property upon death as he chooses.

The other point to remember is that a Will does not come into effect until after the person's death. Up until that time it is merely a piece of paper showing the intention of the person making the Will, who is known as the testator (from the Latin '*testari*' to make a Will, testify). Up until the time of death a Will is not enforceable and can be changed at any time as we shall see.

There are two exceptions to the general rule that anyone can make a Will:

Minors
A minor is a child under the age of eighteen; only a person aged eighteen and over can make a Will that is valid. (But if you are a serviceman you may still be able to make a Will if you are a minor: see Chapter 14, page 143).

Persons of Unsound Mind
A person of unsound mind cannot make a valid Will unless it is shown that the Will was made when the person was experienc-

ing a sane interval. If the person making the Will has been certified (insane) then it is up to the person producing the Will to show that it was made in a sane period. If a person who has made a Will later becomes of unsound mind and/or is certified, then that does not render the Will ineffective so long as he was of sound mind when he made it.

Lastly, where a Will is shown to have been made properly and witnessed properly it is presumed to have been made by a person of sound mind in the absence of evidence to the contrary.

Who, then, is a person of unsound mind? It includes a "defective" which is defined by the Mental Health Act as a person suffering from severe sub-normality which is "a state of arrested or incomplete development of mind which includes sub-normality of intelligence and is of such a nature or degree that the patient is incapable of living an independent life or of guarding himself against serious exploitation, or will be so incapable when of an age to do so". It also includes, generally, a person who has been certified and is detained in a mental hospital.

Foolishness or eccentricity are not enough to establish that a person is of unsound mind, but each case is looked at individually bearing in mind the life and habits of the person making the Will. What in one person might be regarded as merely eccentric might, in another who had never shown any signs of eccentricity, be regarded as mad.

There is one other circumstance which can invalidate a Will which should be mentioned here: that is if it has been induced by fraud, fear, coercion, or excessive pestering.

Fraud arises in the situation where someone wants a person to make a provision in a Will and who tells that person a lie. For fraud to be established the person making the statement must know what he is doing and must know that it is a lie (or not care whether it is a lie or not). He must intend the person making the Will to act upon the lie and the person making the Will must actually do so. Thus, if Mr. Bloggins tells his wife a lie with a view to her leaving him some more money in her Will, and she actually does so, then that provision in the Will may be invalidated.

Similarly, if Mrs. Bloggins threatens her husband with a carving knife and stands over him whilst he makes his Will, or if she nags him about it every morning before breakfast, the provisions may be invalidated.

This, however, differs from excessive flattery or influence which falls short of coercion. In these situations the Will stands: it only comes into question when there is undue influence involving coercion. In a recent case, a man who was suffering from Parkinson's disease drew up his Will only six days before he died. The Will was set aside on the grounds that he did not know or approve of the contents of the Will and was acting under the undue influence of his wife. It was said by the judge that the Will of an old and infirm person ought to be witnessed by a doctor who satisfies himself that the person making the Will is capable of doing so and understands what is written in the Will. The doctor should make a record of his examination and findings.

Foreigners
Since 1870 a foreigner can own land and other property in this country with the exception of a British ship. Consequently, he can leave that property by Will just like any other person of the United Kingdom. Since 1964 there is no distinction between a foreigner and a United Kingdom citizen making a Will in this country.

A permanent move from this country to another country after a Will has been made does not invalidate a Will made in this country according to English law.

Where there is a gift of land and homes in an English Will made in accordance with English law then that gift is not revoked by a clause in a foreign Will made according to foreign law. The same rule applies to a Will made in Scotland according to Scottish law.

A Will of land and homes situated in England will be construed according to English law, whether it is made by a United Kingdom citizen or a foreigner.

A Will of items such as land and homes, and mortgages, leaseholds, interests in freeholds and even debentures representing proceeds of sale of freehold which are situated in another country will be construed according to the law of that country.

The principle is that the disposal of these items is governed by the law of the country in which they are situated.

A Will of items other than these, such as personal effects, is governed by the law of the country in which the person making the Will was last living permanently. Where a person dies living permanently in another country and it is necessary for his Will to be proved in England, then probate will be granted here if the Will was valid under the law of that foreign country.

The general rule, then, is that a Will must conform to the law of the country where it was made or where the person making the Will was living permanently or where (in the case of Wills made in many foreign countries) he was a national, but this is a complicated matter and where these circumstances arise it would be wise to consult a solicitor.

Prisoners
There is no restriction on any prisoner leaving his property by Will or receiving any property under someone else's Will.

Wives
There is no restriction on a married woman leaving her own property by Will.

United Kingdom Citizens Overseas
A Will made by a United Kingdom citizen will be valid if it complies with the law of either

    (i)   the country in which it was made
or (ii) the country in which he intends to make his permanent home
or (iii) the country in which he was living habitually either when the Will was made or at his death
or (iv) the country of which he was a national either when the Will was made or at his death i.e. the United Kingdom. This would mean that a Scottish person could make a Will according to Scottish law, but this can be a complicated matter and you should consult a solicitor if these circumstances arise.

2

WHO CAN BENEFIT FROM A WILL?

In this chapter we consider to which persons and institutions one can leave gifts in a Will.

Death of a Beneficiary
(person to whom a gift is made in a Will)
Sometimes a person to whom property is given in a Will is dead, or dies before the death of the person making the Will.

Usually such a gift is of no effect and the money or property that is given merely becomes part of the residue of the estate (that is what is left of the estate once all the specific gifts in the Will have been made).

Normally it is easy to discover if and when a person has died. but not always.

If for seven years a person has not been heard of by those people who would normally hear from him (such as relatives and business colleagues) and enquiries are made but still no trace of him can be found, then that person is presumed dead in the eyes of the law. The law does not have any rule, however, as to *when* he is meant to have died during those seven years. Suppose Mr. Bloggins leaves his wife and home and goes to South America and nothing is heard from him for seven years, and enquiries in South America do not shed any light on his existence. At the end of the seven years, he will be presumed dead; but there will be no presumption of when he died. If Mrs. Bloggins, therefore, dies two years after he left home there can be no decision as to whether Mr. Bloggins or Mrs. Bloggins died first.

When writing a Will it is always best to think of all eventualities, such as beneficiaries dying before the testator, and to make specific provision for them in the Will. If Bloggins bequeaths "my Picasso collection to Hugh Venables" and Venables dies before Bloggins. then Venables will not receive the Picasso collection which will merely become part of Bloggins' residuary estate. It would be wise, therefore. if there was a clause in Bloggins' Will which gave "my Picasso collection to Hugh Venables and, in the event of Hugh Venables predeceasing me, to his niece Marjorie Venables". This would ensure that someone else had the Picasso collection and it did not merely become part of the residual estate which might mean it was sold.

This is also important because in some circumstances the gift does *not* become part of the residual estate. These exceptions to the general rule are outlined below, and will take effect *unless* there is a clause in the Will to give the gift to someone else, as in the Picasso collection example above.

Exception (i): Gifts to Children
Where a Will contains a devise or bequest to a child or remoter descendant such as a grandchild of the person making the Will and the child (or grandchild) dies before the person making the Will dies then the following occurs. If the child (or grandchild) has a child or children who are living at the time of the death of the person making the Will then the devise or bequest passes to them automatically unless a contrary intention appears in the Will. Likewise, if there is a devise or bequest in a Will to "all my children" (or "all my grandchildren") or to any other class or remoter descendants and one of them dies before the death of the person making the Will then his/her share will pass automatically to his/her child or children if they are living at the time of death of the person making the Will (unless a contrary intention appears in the Will). This provision includes illegitimate children and a child conceived before the death of the person making the Will and born alive thereafter.

Let us look at some examples. Mr. Bloggins in his Will leaves his house, Blackacre, and his stamp collection to his son James. James is married and has a daughter Kathryn aged 25 and his wife is pregnant with Angharad. James dies before Mr. Bloggins. Mr. Bloggins dies before Angharad is born and without changing his Will. Angharad is then born. On Mr. Bloggins' death, and in the absence of any stipulation in his Will to the contrary, Blackacre and his stamp collection do *not* become part of his residuary estate. Instead, both Blackacre and the stamp collection will pass in equal shares to James' children Kathryn and Angharad. Kathryn can take her share immediately but Angharad, being a minor, will have to wait until she is 18 with the property held in trust for her until that age.

To take another example let us assume that Mr. Bloggins leaves £4,000 to be divided equally between his children. They are James, John, Jeremy and Julian. Jeremy has two children Sarah and Sam. Julian has one child Trevor by his wife and, being the rake of the family, an illegitimate child Toby. Mr. Bloggins lives to a ripe old age and both Jeremy and Julian predecease him. Trevor dies before him as well. On Mr. Bloggins' death, he not having changed his Will at all, who receives what? There were four children originally to share £4,000 so each is entitled to £1,000. James and John, both alive at Mr. Bloggins' death, receive their £1,000 each. Jeremy is dead, but he has two children alive at Mr. Bloggins' death so both Sarah and Sam will receive £500 each. Julian is dead and so is Trevor, but Toby is alive at Mr. Bloggins' death, so he will receive £1,000. Had Trevor survived then he and Toby would have shared the £1,000 equally between them.

Exception (ii): Joint Owners
Where property is left in a Will to two or more people as joint owners and one of them dies before the testator, then his share goes to the other surviving joint owner(s).

Mr. Bloggins in his Will leaves Whiteacre jointly to his two brothers Charles and Frederick. Charles dies before Mr. Bloggins, but that does not mean that his half-share merely becomes part of the residue of Mr. Bloggins' estate. Instead, under this exception, Frederick would be entitled to Charles' half-share so that, on Mr. Bloggins' death, Frederick would receive the whole of Whiteacre. More about this in Chapter 3 page 28.

Children
There is no restriction on a gift to the children of the person making the Will and a gift to "children" would include illegitimate children, and adopted children if the Will is made after the formal adoption order. If one wishes to include step-children one should specify these and not just the word "children". See the section on minors on page 21.

Animals
There can be a gift in a Will to look after particular animals such as pets, but it must be stated to be for no longer than 21 years, which is known as the perpetuity rule. Thus Mrs.

Bloggins can leave £1,000 to be held on trust "for the feeding and caring of her pet dog, Fifi, for 21 years if Fifi shall live that long". Gifts to particular animals are not considered to be charitable, however, whereas gifts for the welfare of animals in general may be charitable. The distinction between charitable and non-charitable is important as we shall see later.

Charities

There are important tax concessions to be considered when a gift is given to charity. See Chapter 12, page 134.

Also the rule which disallows gifts as trusts for purposes which appear to go on for ever does not apply if the purpose is a charitable one (see page 26).

If a person wishes to give a gift to charity but cannot decide which charities, this can be done as follows. He can state in his Will that the gift is given to trustees for it to be distributed to charities as the trustees decide. This means that the trustees will select the charities. The person can be satisfied that the gift will go to charity so long as he expresses himself in his Will that the gift is intended solely for charity.

The law relating to charities is far from simple. It is complicated even as to establishing whether a certain institution or purpose is charitable or not. Consequently, it is important to consult a solicitor if you intend to leave a gift to charity in your Will, although a gift to a well-known major charity (such as Oxfam) should be no problem. If you wish to make a gift to an established charity, you should ask them for their standard form of bequest.

What is Charitable?

It is a question of law whether something is charitable or not and this has often come before the courts to decide. They are guided by the fact that in order to be charitable a gift must be for the benefit of the community or of an appreciably important class of the community. An old Act of Parliament in Queen Elizabeth I's time gives an idea of what matters can be regarded as charitable:

> "The relief of aged, impotent and poor people; the maintenance of sick and maimed soldiers and mariners schools of learning, free schools and scholars in universities; the repair of bridges, ports, havens, cause

ways, churches, sea-banks and highways; the education and preferment of orphans; the relief, stock or maintenance for houses of correction; the marriages of poor maids, the supporting, aid and help of young tradesmen, handicraftsmen and persons decayed; the relief or redemption of prisoners or captives; and the aid or ease of any poor inhabitants etc."

In a case in the last century a judge said that the idea of charity could be classified into four divisions:

1. relief of poverty;
2. advancement of education;
3. advancement of religion;
4. other purposes beneficial to the community not falling under any of the other heads.

What if the Charity Ceases to Exist?

It may be that you leave a gift in your Will to a particular charity but it is wound up or ceases to exist before your death. If you wish the gift to go to another charity then you should specify a gift over, for example:

"I bequeath the sum of £500 to ABC charity and, if it has ceased to exist by the date of my death, to XYZ charity."

This still leaves a difficulty, however, if both ABC and XYZ charities cease to exist, or, indeed, never existed at all! Where there is shown in the Will a general charitable intention, then the gift will be applied to an existing charity which has as its objects purposes as close as possible to the charity specified in the Will. What is important is that the Will should contain a general charitable intention. If there is a gift to a charity and you do *not* express a general charitable intention then, if the charity ceases to exist, the gift will merely become part of the residue of the estate and will lose its exemption from Inheritance Tax.

A general charitable intention could be expressed as follows:

"I bequeath the sum of £5,000 to ABC Charity. For the avoidance of doubt I desire that this sum of £5,000 be applied for charitable purposes."

Can My Own Family be a Charitable Purpose?
Yes but this is a most difficult area for Tax Avoidance reasons. If you have this in mind, consult a solicitor.

It has been decided by the courts that a gift for the "maintenance and benefit of any relatives of mine whom my trustees shall consider to be in special need" was a charitable trust. Furthermore, there is nothing to restrict this to relatives living at the date of death. Consequently, it could apply to relatives who are born after the date of death.

When one remembers the important fact that gifts to charities are exempt from Inheritance Tax this may be a way of benefiting one's relatives whilst avoiding tax.

A clause in the Will giving effect to this could be as follows:

> "I bequeath the sum of £500 to A and B to be held on trust for the maintenance and benefit of any relatives of mine whom my trustees shall consider to be in special need and poverty."

Gifts to Animals Which are Charitable Gifts

Gifts to particular animals, such as a pet dog or cat, are not considered to be charitable. Gifts to animals in general, or a species of animal, can be charitable. The test of whether such a gift is charitable or not is not whether it benefits the animals concerned but whether it benefits mankind. This can be by encouraging a more humane attitude towards animals, but, of course, it can be also by assisting mankind in research. A gift will not be considered to be charitable if the overall object does not assist mankind. Consequently, a gift on trust or to a charity whose objects are the prevention of cruelty to animals, such as the R.S.P.C.A., to relieve suffering in animals, such as the P.D.S.A. will be charitable. A gift for the abolition of experiments on animals or to an anti-vivisection society, however, will not be charitable since this in law would be considered to hinder medical research and would not be to the overall benefit of mankind.

Gifts and Racial Discrimination

The legislation dealing with racial discrimination applies to Wills but will not affect any charities whose objects are to benefit people of a certain nationality or ethnic origin etc. Consequently, discrimination in making a gift to a charity for persons who are of a particular ethnic group or race will be lawful. Discrimination *against* people, however, as opposed to discrimination *for* people, is unlawful: it would be unlawful to make a gift to a charity for persons of all races except a particular one.

The situation can be summarised by example:

A gift in trust for the benefit of disabled Jews would be lawful discrimination and allowed.

A gift in trust for the benefit of disabled persons except disabled Jews would be unlawful discrimination and disallowed.

Clubs and Company Employees

A gift to the members of a club who are in poverty is charitable.

A gift to the employees of a company is not charitable unless it is for poor employees.

Gifts to the Aged

A gift for the benefit of the aged is charitable even if there is no mention of poverty. Thus, providing a sheltered home or a day centre or luncheon club for the aged will all be charitable gifts.

Gifts to the Disabled

Likewise, a gift for the benefit of the disabled or incapacitated is charitable even if there is no mention of poverty. This will include gifts to the physically handicapped, the blind, the deaf and dumb, the war disabled and any purpose connected with them such as the provision of a nursing home.

Gifts for the Relief of Poverty

A gift is charitable if it is for the relief of poverty, and this includes words such as destitute, needy, deserving, special need, distress and phrases such as "falling on evil days". Poverty does not mean the bread line. It is a relative term and, consequently, can include people who have moderate means. A gift for the relief of poverty can be charitable if it is only for a certain section of the community and does not have to be for the community as a whole. The following gifts are charitable:—

To the poor persons of a particular town or village.

To the poor persons of a club.

To the poor persons of a regiment or military unit.

To the poor persons of a particular religious group.

To such poor relations as your executor thinks are deserving cases.

A gift to an institution, such as a religious order, is still charitable, if that particular institution works towards the relief of poverty of other persons.

Gifts for the Advancement of Education
These include gifts to particular educational institutions, colleges, universities, etc.: gifts for educating a particular group of people such as the mentally or physically handicapped; and scholarships etc. Such gifts, however, must be for the benefit of the public or a section of the public in order for them to be regarded as charitable.

Gifts for the Advancement of Religion
This includes gifts for religious buildings, churches, graveyards and burial places, religious books, organ and organist, missionaries, clergymen, etc. As in gifts for education, however, there must be a general public benefit arising out of the gift.

Gifts for Other Purposes Beneficial to the Community
This can include gifts which cannot be described under relief of poverty, advancement of education and advancement of religion. The important and essential element in these gifts, however, if they do not come within the other categories, is that they must be for the benefit of the general public and not for individuals.

The following is a list of gifts that have been regarded as being beneficial to the community, but the list is not exhaustive:—

gifts to promote certain ideas
    Conservative principles combined with mental and moral
        improvement
    Socialism
    advancement of ideas of government
gifts for encouraging national feeling
gifts to promote the military and associated purposes
    teaching shooting
    the volunteer corps
    officers' mess
    regimental sport fund

    defence from air attack
    training boys to become Naval or Merchant Naval officers
    prize for cadets
    institutions for ex-members of the forces
gifts for providing accurate law reports
gifts for public works
    building bridges
    protection of the coast
    repairing highways
    public lighting
    hospital
    improvement of a city
    convalescent home for children
    public hall
    public park
    fire brigade
    public library
    public recreation
    museum
gifts for benefiting agriculture.

There are many others, but if you are in doubt you should consult a solicitor for his advice as to whether a particular purpose would be regarded as charitable or not.

Foreigners

A foreigner can receive a gift under the Will. If, however, there is a state of war and he is an enemy then he cannot receive a gift. Likewise, a person who was resident in an enemy country or territory occupied by the enemy would not be able to receive a gift under the Will. It is possible that these people could receive the gift once the war was over.

Minors

A minor is a person who is aged under 18. A minor is not allowed to own land. Consequently no land can be left in a Will to a person who is under the age of 18, at the date of the death of the person making the Will. If one wants to leave land to a minor who may not have reached 18 at the time of one's death then the best method is to give the land to trustees on behalf of a minor.

A minor cannot be a trustee.

While it is the law that minors become of full age at 18 and are then allowed to own land, you may wish to consider whether or not you would wish to insert in your Will a provision that a person should not be entitled to take property under the Will until he/she is rather older, say 23 or 25. If the sums are fairly large, such persons may not have the experience or ability to deal with such a large amount of money until they are older.

Mental Patients
There is no restriction on a gift under a Will being given to a mental patient or to anyone who is not in possession of all their faculties. It may be that someone has to look after the gift because the person receiving it is so unstable in the mind that he could not deal with it. The fact that someone is mentally unstable, however, is no bar to him being left a gift.

Trade Unions and Employers' Associations
Both trade unions and employers' associations are allowed to hold property which is held by trustees on their behalf. It would be wise to contact a solicitor if you are thinking of leaving a gift in your Will to a trade union or employers' association.

Clubs, Societies and Institutions
A gift can be left in a Will to a club or society or other institution whether or not they are charitable. The gift can be expressed to be for the particular institution or, alternatively, it can be expressed to be for the members of the institution.

Companies and Corporations and Local Authorities
There is no restriction on a gift under a Will, including land, being given to a company or corporation or local authority.

Looking After Your Grave After Your Death
Some people will want to have a monument erected or maintained or to have their grave or memorial cared for after their death.

Under an Act of Parliament a burial authority or local authority can agree to maintain:

(a) a grave, vault, tombstone, or other memorial in a burial

ground or crematorium provided or maintained by the
authority;
(b) a monument or other memorial to any person within the
area of the authority to which the authority have right of
access.

If such an agreement is concluded then it cannot be for a
period longer than 99 years. There is no duty on the local
authority to enter into such an agreement and it is a matter for
the local authority to decide whether it wishes to enter into
such an agreement or not.

If a person wants such an agreement whereby the local
authority will maintain a grave or monument then he should
direct in his Will that his executors should enter into such an
agreement with the local authority. He should ensure also that
there is sufficient money for the local authority to be paid.

This applies to *any* grave, monument, memorial, etc. and
not just to that of the person making the Will.

Bankrupt Beneficiary

It may be that you wish to leave property in your Will to a
person who is either bankrupt or in danger of becoming
bankrupt, such as somebody whose business has fallen on bad
times, or even a spendthrift son! Your greatest concern, of
course, will be to try to ensure that your money does not go
directly to the creditors. This can be done by leaving your
property or money on a "protective trust".

A "protective trust" means that the person in whose favour
it is made has an interest in the property for a certain period
and thereafter, the property is distributed amongst himself and
his near relatives at the discretion of the trustees.

Thus, if you wish to leave £10,000 to your son, but you are
worried in case he becomes bankrupt after your death and it all
goes to the estate in bankruptcy, you could phrase it like this:

"I bequeath £10,000 to my son Harold upon protective
trust for his life."

This would have the effect that if Harold never became
bankrupt then he would enjoy the income from the £10,000 for
the rest of his life after which the money would be divided
among his estate and his near relatives at the discretion of the
trustees. If Harold became bankrupt, however, the money
would not go for the benefit of his creditors. Instead it would be
divided up among his wife, if he has one, and his children, if he

has any. If he has neither wife nor children then it would be divided up among those who would be entitled to it if he were dead.

You might feel that your son is in danger of becoming bankrupt up to a certain age, but after that age his profligate ways will change. If you feel that he will be beyond danger after the age of 25 you might leave a protective trust for a shorter period:

> "I bequeath £10,000 to my son Harold upon protective trust until he reach the age of 25."

This would mean that if he does not become bankrupt before 25 Harold would have the income from the £10,000 until he reached 25. The £10,000 would then be divided up among himself, wife and children, if he has any, at the discretion of the trustees.

If Harold becomes bankrupt before the age of 25, he loses his absolute entitlement to the money and the £10,000 may be divided up, at the Trustees' discretion, among his wife and children, if he has any, or among those who would be entitled to his property on his death if he has neither wife nor children. A way in which he could be given a second chance is to create two (or more) protective trusts, say, one until he reached the age of 25, and another one for life.

The dividing up is done at the discretion of the trustees, so it is important to appoint trustees in the Will if you wish to leave property on protective trusts.

If your son is bankrupt already at the time of making your Will then you can still leave him property on protective trusts. You should make clear, however, that you know he is bankrupt and that you wish your trustees to divide up the property at their discretion on your death. It may be, of course, that your son is declared bankrupt at one stage after you have made your Will, but is discharged before your death. If there are protective trusts the position is still safeguarded if he becomes bankrupt again after your death.

If you are considering any of these courses of action you would be wise to consult a solicitor.

Who Cannot Benefit Under the Will?
Witnesses to the Will
The signature of a person making a Will has to be witnessed by

two persons (unless the person making the Will is a serviceman: see Chapter 14, page 144). Those two people, or their husbands or wives, are not allowed to take any gift in the Will and, if there is a gift to a person who has acted as a witness to the signature, or to his/her husband/wife or any person claiming under them, then that gift fails and it becomes part of the residual estate of the person making the Will. This only applies to any gifts in the Will to a witness, his/her husband/wife and any person claiming under them, it does not apply to any charge or debt owing to them from the estate for which direction as to payment is given in the Will. Thus it would not apply to a gift of property to Bloggins so that he could hold it on trust for the benefit of baby Bloggins. The gift would not fail, although Bloggins had witnessed the signature, because the gift was not for himself but was for baby Bloggins.

A person who is given a gift in a Will can nevertheless witness the signature to a codicil of the Will (see page 43) so long as he does not receive anything under the codicil.

So long as there are two persons who have witnessed the signature to a Will and who do not receive any gifts in it then it does not matter if other people who do receive gifts in the Will also witness the signature. These people will still be able to receive their gifts, even though they witnessed the signature, so long as there are also two witnesses who do not receive any gifts. It is advisable, however, not to complicate matters and merely to have two witnesses neither of whom receive anything in the Will.

Killing the Person Making the Will

It used to be the law that under no circumstances could a person who had unlawfully killed, or aided or abetted or procured the death of, the person making the Will benefit from its provisions. This is called the "forfeiture rule" but has now been modified. Where the forfeiture rule would otherwise preclude a person from receiving any property under a Will then the Court can make an order allowing a person to receive the property if it considers that, in the circumstances, the justice of the case demands it. This might apply, for example, where a person is convicted of manslaughter of the testator, or killing him in a car crash where there was no intention to harm or kill him. Such an application to the Court, however, must be made within three months of the conviction. This does *not* apply, however, to a murderer. Where a person is convicted of the murder of the testator then the forfeiture rule takes effect without any possible modification and he can receive nothing under the Will. The forfeiture rule does not preclude anyone from making a claim under the Inheritance (Provision for Family and Dependants) Act 1975, for which you should read Chapter 10, page 113).

Fraud, Fear, Coercion and Excessive Pestering
We have seen in Chapter 1 (page 10) the sort of activity that can amount to coercion, pestering and fraud. If any of these things have been done by a beneficiary under the Will then a gift to him can be set aside.

Gifts For Purposes Which Go On For Ever
Where a gift is non-charitable then the law will not uphold it if it is likely to go on for ever. If I left in my Will the sum of £10,000 to be held on trust and the income used to paint my front door every year, then, in the absence of a limit of the number of years that this should go on it could go on for ever. The law will normally not allow this, since it is felt that there should be a time in the foreseeable future when the £10,000 should be used up.

3

WHAT PROPERTY CAN BE DEALT WITH IN A WILL?

In this Chapter we consider what is meant by legacies and what property a testator can leave in his Will to others.

Your Body
The executors can have the final say in the disposal of a body after death because the law does not recognise any property in a dead body and, consequently, no provision in the Will can bind the executors. Nevertheless, it is normal for there to be a

clause in the Will dealing with the disposal of the body, whether by burial or cremation, which usually is respected by the executors.

In addition to the method of disposal of the body there can be a direction in a Will as to the funeral arrangements, maintenance of the grave or where ashes should be scattered and what gravestone or monument should be set up.

People are becoming increasingly aware of the value to medicine of leaving their body, or part of their body, either for purposes of medical science or for spare-part surgery. A person making a Will can leave any part of his body including eyes, heart and kidneys to be used for spare-part surgery or other therapeutic uses, or for medical research. He can do this either in writing or by a declaration in the presence of two witnesses during the illness from which he dies.

Many people now carry a kidney donor card which can be obtained from most doctors' surgeries or hospitals. This is a very worthwhile way of helping someone after death as there is a shortage of kidneys for transplant. A kidney donor card authorises the use of kidneys for this purpose and should be always carried on the person as time is critical after death.

Obviously, for the purposes of spare-part surgery the particular organs must be removed shortly after death. The person who is entitled to possession of the body, usually the next-of-kin, can authorise the removal of eyes unless he believes that the dead person had an objection or the surviving spouse or other relative objects. The removal is done by a doctor who must have satisfied himself that the person is dead. Where a person dies in hospital then an officer of the hospital can authorise removal if the dead person expressed his desire that this was his wish either in writing or by a declaration in the presence of two witnesses during the illness from which he died.

Because eyes have to be removed within a few hours of death it is always better for the person dying to give a spoken authorisation during the last illness in addition to giving a direction in the Will. If there is such a direction in the Will then it is, of course, essential for the fact to be made known to the person who can do something about it on the death. If the direction is in the Will but no one except the dying person knows it, then, by the time the Will is read, it is too late to be of any value.

Those who are considering leaving their eyes, or any other

part of the body would be wise to contact the nearest hospital
or local doctor for further information.

With all organs it is important that decisions should be made
swiftly upon death.

Leaving Your Body for Medical Research

The local hospital will be able to advise suitable arrangements
for those who wish to leave their body for the purposes of
medical education. It is better not to specify a particular
medical school or institution, because no one can tell where the
body might be needed for examination at the time of death.

The surviving husband or wife or nearest relative can object
to a person's body being used in this way and can ask for burial
or cremation without this happening.

Before the body can be removed for these purposes a death
certificate and a notice to the Inspector of Anatomy must be
completed. The procedure is for the next-of-kin to contact
immediately the Inspector of Anatomy in London, or the
Professor of Anatomy at the nearest medical school, who will
arrange to have the body collected and will provide the forms if
they have not been obtained already.

There is often a fear that if one leaves one's body for medical
science or therapeutics there is a danger that removal of organs
might commence by mistake when the person is still alive. Such
a fear is groundless since, under the Human Tissue Act, 1961,
no removal of any organ can take place until a registered
medical practitioner has satisfied himself that death has
occurred.

In any event, a person may wish to have his body examined
by other persons after his death to ensure that he will not be
buried alive. The expenses of this examination would be paid
out of the estate.

Land and Buildings

A person may dispose in his Will of any *freehold* land or houses
of which he is the sole owner. If he is a *joint owner* (not a tenant
in common), however, such as where a husband and wife buy a
property in joint names, then he *cannot* in his Will dispose of
his half share. In such a case the half share goes to the other
joint owner who survives. The principle is the same where there
are several, say four, joint owners. When one dies, he cannot
dispose of his quarter share because it goes to the other three. If
another one dies then his third share goes to the other two, and

when one of these two dies, as we have seen, his half share goes to the sole survivor.

It is essential to keep a Will up to date because when a person dies he may own more property than he did at the time of making his Will or he may have disposed of property between making his Will and his death. Thus if he is a joint owner but all the other joint owners die before him then he is able to dispose of the whole of the property in his Will, even if at the time of making his Will he was one of many joint owners. If the other joint owners die before him it would be prudent to make another Will disposing of all the property.

Likewise, if Bloggins owns Blackacre and makes his Will leaving it to his son but afterwards sells Blackacre to Mrs. Periwinkle, then on Bloggins' death his son will not receive Blackacre because, at the time of Bloggins' death, it no longer belonged to Bloggins and so was not capable of disposal by him.

Not all property is freehold. Many properties, such as flats, are leasehold. The holder of a leasehold can dispose of it in his Will just as he can dispose of his freehold. The only difference is that the executor may need to get the consent of the freehold owner of the leasehold premises. For example, if I am the leaseholder of a 99 year lease on a flat, the freehold of which is owned by ABC Property Company Limited, then in my Will I may leave the flat to Mr. Bloggins. Suppose, however, in my lease between ABC Property Company Limited and myself there is a clause that states I shall not assign the lease without the consent of ABC Property Company Limited. Then, on my death, before Mr. Bloggins can receive the leasehold of the flat my executor will have to seek the permission of ABC Property Company Limited.

Other property may not be in fact in the possession of the person making the Will, but if he is entitled to it then he can dispose of it in his own Will. Such a situation arises when a person in his Will leaves someone else some property and the second person is aware of this, in which case the second person can make a gift of the property in his own Will. If Mrs. Bloggins leaves Blackacre in her Will to her son James, then James can make a Will while his mother is still alive in which he can leave Blackacre to his friend Simon, although at the time of making the Will he does not actually have possession of Blackacre, since at that time it is still in Mrs. Bloggins' ownership. When Mrs. Bloggins dies Blackacre will pass to James and he will then have possession of it. If James dies before his mother then Simon may still get Blackacre provided Mrs. Bloggins' Will enables it to pass to the person whom James should appoint in the event of him predeceasing her.

Where a person owns *agricultural land* then any crops growing on it or livestock grazing on it will usually be included in a gift of the land itself unless there is a separate gift of the crops and/or livestock.

Insurance Policies

Very much depends upon the terms of the insurance policy as to whether money which is to be paid under it can, in fact, be disposed of in a Will. Such terms should be carefully scrutinised. If there are no terms restricting the person who can receive money payable under a policy, nor a specified person such as the husband or wife, or group of persons who are entitled, then a person who took out the policy of insurance on his own life can dispose of the money payable in his Will.

Shares

Subject to any restriction placed upon the disposal of shares by the Company (common in Private Companies), any shares can be disposed of in a Will just like any other property.

Money

Gifts of money in a Will are usually called pecuniary legacies.

Specific Items

Specific items can be disposed of in a Will. Unless items are specifically mentioned in a Will, they become part of the estate and can be sold to satisfy pecuniary legacies.

Property Abroad

A Will disposing of property that is situated abroad generally will be governed by the law of the country in which the property is situated. You should seek the advice of a solicitor if you have property abroad which you wish to include in your Will.

Legacies

In general terms a legacy is merely another name for a gift of an item or money, but not of land. Where there is a gift of money this is called a pecuniary legacy.

There is a distinction to be made between gifts of specific items and gifts of money, and this can be quite important, especially if you have made a miscalculation as to the extent and value of your property and, in your Will, you leave more than you have actually got.

In these circumstances, the rules give effect to the gifts of specific items before the gifts of money, so that some of those who have been given money may be disappointed.

Likewise, if you make gifts in your Will which leave insufficient money with which to pay your debts, funeral expenses and the cost of the administration of your Will, then the money for these expenses and costs will be taken from pecuniary legacies and not legacies of specific items. Consequently, the person to whom you have given a gift of money may be disappointed.

A gift of a specific item means a gift in the Will which clearly identifies the item. Thus, a gift of "a ring" is not a specific gift because it could refer to any ring. In order to make it a specific gift you would have to identify it further, such as a gift of "my sapphire ring with the twisted gold surround".

Hopefully, the situation in which some beneficiaries of pecuniary legacies would be disappointed will not arise. You can ensure this by making certain that you have not given more than you have got, that you have made allowance for payment of your debts, funeral expenses, Inheritance Tax, and the expenses of administration, and by leaving a residue of your estate out of which any such further payments can be made.

4

WHAT HAPPENS IF I DO NOT MENTION ALL MY PROPERTY IN MY WILL?

The situation may arise where a person does not dispose of all his property in the Will. This may be intentional or it may be merely an oversight because he did not know that he had the property, or simply that he did not have the property at the time he made the Will.

Any property that is not disposed of by the Will is sold and the proceeds of sale are used to pay funeral and administration expenses, debts and other liabilities. Any further proceeds are used to pay any gifts of money under the Will and anything left over after that is distributed according to the law of intestacy, that is as if there had not been a Will (see Chapter 8, page 108).

When we say that any property is sold that is not specifically disposed of in the Will, this is subject to one exception. Personal items are not sold unless the money is needed to pay for administration. (Personal items mean carriages, horses, stable furniture and effects (which are not used for business purposes), motor cars and accessories (which are not used for business purposes), garden effects, domestic animals, plate, plated articles, linen, china, glass, books, pictures, prints, furniture, jewellery, which includes unmounted stones, articles of household or personal use which include a motor yacht and a stamp collection, ornaments, musical and scientific instruments and apparatus, wines, liquors and consumable stores. Personal items do not mean any articles used for business purposes nor money or securities for money.)

Let us say that Mr. Bloggins owns Whiteacre worth £60,000, Blackacre worth £38,000, a motor car worth £10,000, a set of Waterford glass goblets worth £1,000, his work tools worth £500 and a piano. In his Will he leaves Whiteacre to his wife. He leaves his piano and a legacy of £35,500 to his son. He forgets that he owns Blackacre or anyway makes no mention of it, nor of the motor car, nor of the Waterford glass goblets, nor of his tools in his Will. The funeral expenses and expenses of administration of the estate come to £3,000 altogether.

Applying the rules set out above Blackacre will be sold. £3,000 of the proceeds of sale will go to pay the funeral and administration expenses. This leaves £35,000 which will go towards the legacy to his son. The extra £500 to make up the £35,500 legacy to his son will be found from the sale of his tools for £500. Since these were used for his business purposes they are not classified as personal items. His son will also receive the piano which has been left to him specifically. The motor car and Waterford glass goblets are personal items. It is not necessary to sell them to pay for administration costs, consequently, they will not be sold but will be given to his wife under the rules of the law of intestacy. (This example ignores any liability to pay Inheritance Tax, which also will have to be taken into consideration.)

Of course the problem of property not being mentioned in the Will need not arise at all if the precaution is taken of dealing with the *residue* of the estate in the Will itself, for example by the inclusion of such a clause as:

"I devise and bequeath the residue of my real and personal estate to my wife Anne Belinda Bloggins absolutely."

5

HOW CAN MY WILL BE MADE INOPERATIVE?

A Will can be made inoperative, or revoked, as it is called, either by choice or accident or external events. The following events have this effect:

1. Making a new valid Will. This does not always have the effect of revoking an earlier Will. If you wish to be sure that the first Will is superseded by the later one then you should destroy the first one, or state specifically in the later one that all previous Wills of yours are revoked.

2. Becoming married after making the Will. Your marriage to someone subsequent to signing your Will has the effect of revoking it and you should then make a new Will. This, however, requires qualification. If there is a provision in the Will, for example, which is exercising a power of appointment, then that takes effect even after marriage unless the property involved would otherwise pass to the personal representatives of the person making the Will. Secondly, where it appears from a Will that at the time of making it the person was expecting to be married to a particular person and intended that the Will should not be revoked by the marriage then the Will remains valid after the marriage. This applies to all the provisions of the Will unless it appears from the Will that there was an intention by the person making it that any particular provision should be revoked by the marriage. As we can see, the important thing is to make it quite clear in the Will that you are intending to marry a particular person and want the Will to remain valid after the marriage. Otherwise, the marriage will have the effect of revoking the Will. If in any doubt it is safest to make a new Will. You should read Chapter 9, page 111.

3. Divorce after making the Will. This includes the situation where a Court annuls a marriage or declares it void after the making of the Will. In such circumstances the Will takes effect unaltered save that any appointment of the former spouse as an executor or trustee is treated as though it were omitted altogether. In addition, any devise or bequest to the former

33

spouse has no effect. This is unless there is a contrary intention expressed in the Will. This, however, does not affect the right of a former spouse to apply for financial provision under the Inheritance (Provision for Family and Dependants) Act 1975 for which you should read Chapter 10, page 113. In addition, this has the effect that if property in the Will is subject to a life interest in favour of the former spouse then it passes automatically to the person who is entitled to it ultimately, as though there had been no life interest. Very often, for example, the person making the Will gives a life interest in his property to his wife with it going to his children after her death. If he divorces his wife and the Will remains unaltered then all that happens is that the children become entitled absolutely to the property on his death and the divorced wife is cut out altogether.

4. *Not complying with the formalities required for making a Will*. See Chapter 6, page 35. A failure to comply with these requirements will render the Will inoperative. For example, it is essential that the Will is written and your signature witnessed by two persons (unless you are a serviceman or a mariner in which case see Chapter 14, page 144).

5. *Destruction of the Will*. This can be done by the person who made the Will or by some other person in his presence and under his direction. The Will is revoked by burning, tearing, or otherwise destroying it. In addition, the person who made the Will must intend that the Will should be revoked.

You cannot revoke a Will merely by crossing it through or drawing a line across it, or even writing "all these are revoked" on it. There must be some burning, tearing or other destruction. It is sufficient to revoke the whole Will if the signature of the person making it is either erased or cut off. It is also sufficiently revoked if the signatures of the witnesses are erased or cut off. If a part of a Will is destroyed then that revokes only that part of the Will and not all of the Will unless the signatures are erased or cut off, in which case the whole Will is revoked. The destruction of a Will does not revoke a codicil to the Will. The codicil must be destroyed separately. However, codicils should be avoided anyway.

In order for a Will to be revoked by destruction there must be an intention to revoke the Will by the person who made it. Accidental destruction, therefore, does not revoke the Will. An example will explain more clearly:

If Mr. Bloggins throws his Will on the fire with the intention that it should no longer be effective, then the Will is revoked, if it is, in fact, burnt.

If, however, Mr. Bloggins sweeps up some old papers from his desk which he wishes to throw away and, by mistake, his Will is amongst them, then that Will is not revoked even though he accidentally throws it on the fire with the other old papers.

If a person tears up a Will when he is mad or drunk, then it will not be revoked by his action.

Thus, for a Will to be revoked in this way there must be both an act of destruction together with the intention to revoke it.

A Will that is accidentally lost is not revoked. One word of warning, however: if a Will is kept in your possession and it cannot be found at your death then it may be presumed to have been destroyed by you with the intention of destroying it, so that it is taken to have been revoked. This should be carefully considered when you decide upon where to keep your Will.

Where a Will cannot be found at your death it is not presumed to have been destroyed with the intention of revoking it if there is evidence of its contents and the testator's declarations. Such evidence could be a photocopy of the Will, so it might be sensible to keep a photocopy in another place in case the original Will cannot be found at your death.

6

THE FORM OF THE WILL

A Will is a formal document and there are certain requirements which must be complied with in order to ensure that it will take effect. It is important therefore, to read this chapter especially carefully.

Provided that these rules are adhered to there is nothing particularly difficult in drafting a Will and it is certainly within most people's capabilities. If, however, you are worried about tax considerations or have complicated affairs then you would be well advised to go to a solicitor for advice.

Apart from the formalities, keep uppermost in your mind that you must express yourself clearly and unambiguously in the Will. Remember that when the Will is read you will not be around to help to interpret it. A good test, once you have written the Will, is to read it through yourself as though you were coming to it fresh and see if it adequately covers your intentions. Better still, ask someone else to read it and get them to tell you what they think it means and see if their view coincides with what you intend it to mean. If it does not then you should write it again in clearer language.

Obviously, your choice of words is critical. Certain words in English can mean different things so, if you are unsure about the meaning of a word, you should either avoid it and use another word or words or else look it up in the dictionary. It may be that the person who has the job of reading and interpreting your Will, your executor, will have to rely upon the definition given in the Oxford Dictionary. There should be no need for this, however, so long as your words and intentions are clear. As a guide, there is set out later in this chapter the likely way in which certain words would be interpreted.

Finally, in order to help you draft your Will, there are examples of Wills which cover many situations, and these can be found in the next chapter.

The Court now has wide powers to rectify the Will so as to make it accord with the testator's intentions if it fails to do so as a result of a clerical error or a failure to understand his instructions. You should read Chapter 10, page 112.

Writing

Your Will can be written on any material, although, obviously, paper is preferable.

It can be typed, printed, lithographed or hand-written. Parts of it can be in one manner whilst other parts in another manner so that, for example, the main body of the Will could be typed whilst blank spaces can be filled in by hand by writing. It is better that a Will should be typed rather than hand-written simply because there will be no confusion over words when it is read whereas some hand-writing can be almost indecipherable.

If the Will is hand-written then it is important that it should be legible. Special rules apply to a hand-written Will in Scotland (see Chapter 13, page 140). A hand-written Will can be made in either ink or pencil, but ink is preferable. Never mix ink and pencil, because this will have the effect of making the ink parts valid and the pencil parts not valid. Likewise, if a Will is made in ink never make alterations in pencil, because the pencilled alterations will have no effect, since they will be regarded as merely ideas of alteration rather than firm alterations. See "Alterations", page 42.

International Wills
What is the situation if a person owns property in several countries and wants to make a Will? On 26th October, 1973 the Convention on International Wills at Washington concluded a uniform law on the form of an International Will. This means that a Will can be dealt with in the United Kingdom irrespective of the place where it was made, of the location of the assets and of the nationality and place of residence of the person making it so long as it complies with the following requirements:-

1. It is in writing.
2. It need not be written by the person making it.
3. It may be written in any language, by hand or by any other means.
4. The person making it must declare in the presence of two witnesses and a solicitor that the document is his Will and that he knows the contents, but he need not inform them of the contents.
5. In the presence of the two witnesses and the solicitor the person making the Will must sign it, or acknowledge his signature if he has signed it already, and the witnesses and the solicitor must sign in his presence there and then. All the signatures must be at the end of the Will and each sheet must be signed by the person making the Will and numbered if there is more than one sheet.
6. The date of the Will is the date of its signature by the solicitor who must note it at the end of the Will.
7. The solicitor then attaches to the Will a certificate in a prescribed form and mentioning in it the place where the person making it intends to keep it, if he wishes.

At the time of writing this book the provisions for International Wills had not yet been brought into effect but were expected to be brought into operation in the near future. You should check this.

Printed Will Forms
You can go to a law stationers and many bookshops and buy printed Will forms for a few pence. Some people prefer to use these and they can be very helpful, especially as many have instructions which are easily understandable on how to make the Will. On these forms there are printed the important phrases and then there are large blank spaces for you to fill in with your wishes and information on your property. On these forms or on any Will it does not matter if blank spaces are left. You do not *have* to fill them in with lines just because there is more space than you need. One word of caution here. It is always better, though not essential, to leave no blank spaces so as to ensure that no additional insertions can be made in your Will without your knowledge. This can be done by ruling through any blank spaces. If there is not enough room on the form for all your requirements, then attach a further sheet, but make sure it is correctly signed and witnessed *at the end*.

Signature
Every Will must be signed by the person making it, or by some other person in his presence and by his direction. Either this must be done in the presence of two or more witnesses who are present at the same time or the person making the Will can sign it and then get two or more witnesses, who must be present at the same time, to acknowledge his signature on the Will. Two witnesses are enough. Each witness must sign the Will in the presence of the person making it, but not necessarily in the presence of any other witness.

There is no requirement that the signature of the person making the Will should be at the end of it or at the foot of the page but it is better to sign it at the end because the law requires that, for a Will to be valid, it should appear that by his signature the person making it intended to give effect to it. Likewise, the time of signing the Will is important because anything inserted in the Will after the signature has been made will have no effect. Once you have signed your Will, with the signature witnessed by two witnesses, then if you wish to change it you should destroy it completely and start again.

Where the Will consists of several pages it is not necessary to sign all the pages; but all the pages should be attached to one another in some way, for example, by string. However, to avoid doubt, it is safer for each separate sheet of paper to be signed at the foot by you and the two witnesses. It is preferable that the Will is written on a single piece of paper, perhaps a very large piece that is folded down the middle.

Form of Signature

This should be your usual signature. There is still a valid signature if there is merely a mark, such as a cross, and it is unnecessary to show that the person making the mark cannot write. A thumb print has been accepted. It is obvious, however, that signature is best and this should be a full usual signature. Placing a seal on the Will is not sufficient, but initials and signature by a rubber stamp have been accepted. Although a signature can be made in pencil even when the rest of the Will is in ink it is not good practice and you should sign in ink. Although it is best that you should sign in your proper name, it is all right if you sign in another name so long as that is intended to be your name. Thus, an actor can sign in his stage name or a woman can sign in her maiden name or the name of her first marriage.

Blind or Illiterate Persons

A blind or illiterate person can have the Will signed by someone else on his/her behalf. This can be anyone, even one of the two witnesses, and so long as it is expressed to be on behalf of the person making the Will, it can be his own name that he signs on behalf of the person making the Will. It should be stated in terms such as these "Signed on behalf of and in the presence of John Bloggins" where John Bloggins is the person making the Will. Of course, a blind person can sign his own Will by signature or by making a mark if he is shown where, or his hand is guided to the place where the signature should be. There is one further matter: in the case of blind or illiterate persons it must be shown that they were aware of the contents of the Will. This is satisfied usually by one of the witnesses certifying that he has read the Will over to the person making the Will and that the person making the Will seemed to understand it in words such as these: "I (full names) certify that I have read the whole of this Will to (full names of testator) and I further certify that I am satisfied that he/she seemed to understand it."

Foreigners
Where a person is a foreigner one of the witnesses should
certify that the Will has been read over to or by the person
making the Will and that the person making the Will either
seemed to understand it (if he/she has a working knowledge of
English) or that it was translated into his/her native language.

Witnesses
Every Will must be signed by the person making it, or his
signature must be acknowledged, in the presence of two or
more witnesses. Two are enough. Both witnesses must be
present at the same time which is the time the person making
the Will actually signs it or acknowledges his signature. Both
witnesses must then sign the Will in the presence of the person
making it, but one witness does not have to be present when the
other one is signing it so long as both have been present at the
time the person making it signed it or acknowledged his
signature. The point is that each of the two witnesses should be
able to say that to his/her knowledge the person making the
Will actually signed it. Consequently, a blind person cannot be
a witness.

Moreover, the person making the Will must sign the Will
before the two witnesses add their signatures. Both witnesses
must be present at that time and they must both sign in the
presence of the person making the Will, who must be aware of
what they are doing.

Witnesses have the choice of signing either to the effect that
the testator has signed the Will in their presence or to the effect
that they acknowledge that the signature on the Will is that of
the testator.

It is not necessary for the witnesses to know what is in the
Will nor to read the Will, unless the person making the Will is
blind or illiterate and needs to have it read out loud. The
witnesses' sole real function is to see the person making the
Will sign it. There is provision for the person making the Will
to sign it and then come to the witnesses and acknowledge in
front of the two witnesses that it is his/her signature. It is safest,
however, for the person making the Will actually to sign it in
the presence of the two witnesses.

Each witness must attest and sign the Will. Although no
form of attestation is necessary it is safest for the witnesses to
put their signatures against a brief clause stating that the Will

was signed by the testator (the person making the Will) or he acknowledged his signature in the presence of the two witnesses who were present at the time and in the presence of each other and who signed themselves in the testator's presence. You can see this in the samples in Chapter 7.

Signature of the Witnesses

This can be by initials or a mark, but it should be by the usual full signature of the persons. The signature can even be by a rubber stamp which merely stamps his name and not even a facsimile of his signature, but he must have taken some physical part, such as actually using the stamp himself to place his name on the Will. This sort of activity, however, is strongly discouraged and the usual signature should be used.

Strictly speaking, the witnesses' signatures can be on any part of the Will so long as it is apparent that they were witnessing the signature of the person making the Will. Unlike the signature of the person making the Will the witnesses' signatures do not *have* to be at the foot of the Will. If they are not, however, it may well complicate matters. It is best to ensure that the witnesses' signatures come just below the signature of the person making the Will.

Who Can be a Witness?

As we have seen, a blind person cannot witness a signature. In general, anyone can be a witness to a person's signature on a Will. If the witness is the blackest rogue around it does not invalidate the Will. From a practical point-of-view, however, it is preferable to have as witnesses people who are of good standing, honest and creditable so that it is unlikely that allegations of fraud or improper behaviour will be made.

It is most important to note that the persons who act as the two witnesses cannot receive any money or gift under the Will. Consequently, you should take care that you do not have as the two witnesses any beneficiaries (persons who receive gifts under the Will) or any of your executors to whom you have given a legacy, or to whom you have specifically authorised payment of fees or charges. It also applies to the spouses (husbands or wives) of such executors and beneficiaries so that if they or their husbands/wives witness the testator's signature they will not be able to receive anything.

How Many Witnesses?
You should have only two witnesses. Only two are necessary, and if you have more then it can complicate matters. Where there are more than two witnesses then any witnesses (or their spouses) who are executors or beneficiaries *will* be able to receive money or property under the Will *so long as* in addition there are two witnesses who are not executors or beneficiaries or their spouses.

Witness to the Capacity of the Testator
Where the question is raised as to whether the person making the Will had the mental capacity or not to be able to make the Will, then this is a matter which is decided by the courts which hear all the relevant evidence. It is not really a consideration of the two witnesses, but where it is thought that the mental ability of a person to make a Will may be called into question then it is desirable to have a doctor as one of the two witnesses. This is especially important, perhaps, where the person making the Will is suffering from mental disorder but actually makes the Will in what is known as a lucid interval when he/she is all right.

Alterations
Preferably, these should be made in ink. Alternatively, they could be made by pasting over certain parts of the Will or by erasing and retyping parts of the Will. If you are typing your Will you must be careful not to make any mistakes.

Alterations are strongly discouraged, but, if they are made, they must be signed, either by signature or by initials, by the person making the Will and the two witnesses. You must be careful to remember this requirement, as an alteration will not take effect unless either opposite or near to it appear the signatures of the person making the Will and the two witnesses. These signatures can appear on a memorandum referring to the alteration, but it is better that the signatures should be as close as possible to the alteration.

Finally, do not forget that *any* alteration, however made, will not take effect if it is made *after* the time that the person making the Will has signed the Will itself.

If you make a mistake writing the Will, re-write it and scrap the old one rather than have any alterations in it.

Stamp Duty and Seal
There is no need for a stamp or seal to appear on a Will.

Codicil
A codicil is a later addition or alteration to your Will which is a separate document for the drafting of which formalities are required, similar to those necessary for drafting a Will. You are strongly advised not to try to alter your Will by a codicil as this can be very complicated. It is much better to scrap the original Will altogether and to write out another one if you wish to alter it at any time later on.

Additional Documents
When drafting your Will you can refer to other documents and they will be included as part of the Will even though they have not had the formalities of a Will such as signature and witnesses, subject to the following conditions.

A document will be treated as part of the Will if:
1) It is referred to in the Will;
2) The reference to it in the Will is sufficient to be able to identify that particular document; and
3) The document is in existence at the time of making the Will and is not a document that will come into existence at a later date.

Recital
There may be some matters which you wish to have included in your Will which do not directly deal with your property but which are statements of your feelings or intentions. There is no reason why you should not include such a statement which is known as a recital. The following are the kinds of recital you may wish to make:

1. Expression of Affection Towards Someone or Recognition of Your Moral Indebtedness to Someone
This is particularly useful if you decide not to make any gift to a particular person but do not want him to think that he has been left out of the Will either deliberately or by mistake. Such a situation could arise in which one daughter has spent much of her life looking after you in your old age whereas the other daughter has married and had children and is well provided for by her husband. In such a case you might wish to leave

everything to the daughter who has devoted her life to you, but at the same time do not wish to cause resentment in the other daughter by not mentioning her at all. To satisfy this there could be a clause in your Will like this:

"I hereby declare that I hold my daughter Anita Periwinkle in permanent and great affection and I make this Will as a result of my belief that she is well provided for by her husband."

You could add your feelings of gratitude towards the daughter who has cared for you like this:—

"I make this Will in recognition of my gratitude and affection towards my daughter Benita Bloggins who has cared for me in my ailing years."

2. General Charitable Intention

As explained fully in Chapter 2, page 17, you may wish to express a general charitable intention, which could be expressed like this:—

"I bequeath the sum of £5000 to the XYZ Society and, for the avoidance of doubt, I hereby declare that I desire the said sum of £5000 to be given to charity in any event."

3. Statement of Existing Circumstances

This can be done to explain a particular gift and to clarify matters.

If Bertie Bloggins lends me £1000 interest free and I agree to repay him by leaving him £1000 in my Will I could do this by merely stating in my Will "I bequeath the sum of £1000 free of tax to Bertie Bloggins". There is no mention that it is a repayment of the loan and, if Bertie Bloggins was unscrupulous, he could receive the £1000 and still claim that he was owed £1000 as a repayment of his loan. In this case he stands to get a further £1000 out of my estate if his claim is successful. In these circumstances it would be sensible to set out the reason for my giving Bertie Bloggins £1000 and it could be done like this:—

"I bequeath the sum of £1000 free of tax to Bertie Bloggins in satisfaction and repayment of an interest-free loan of £1000 by him to me during my lifetime."

In certain circumstances it may be helpful to set out your beliefs as to the state of your family at the time of making the Will, although any statements in a Will should be avoided unless they are really necessary. The more you say in loose

statements in a Will the more may be ambiguous and likely to
upset the whole Will.

Where you have been given a power to do something or
appoint someone, for example under a settlement, then you
should set out in the Will what you are entitled to do. Thus, if
there is a settlement which was made on your marriage in
which you are given the power to distribute the funds amongst
your children, then you should state this as well as your
intention. It could be written like this:

> "Whereas by a settlement dated . . . and executed on my
> marriage with my husband John Bloggins a power of
> appointing the trust funds of the said settlement among
> the children of my said marriage in such shares as I
> should think fit was given to me I hereby appoint and
> direct that . . ."

Certainty

It cannot be stressed sufficiently strongly that some of the
greatest problems in interpreting Wills can arise out of
ambiguity and can frustrate the intention of the person making
the Will. It is critical, therefore, that the words and phrases
used should be clear and unambiguous. Where a gift is uncertain
it may not take effect on your death.

Persons

When referring to persons you should use their full names and,
if they have a relationship to you then that should be stated as
well. Do not just refer to "my wife" or "Mary Bloggins" but
"my wife Mary Bloggins", and this is so for all relationships. If
you have two nephews named John and you wish to make a
gift to a particular one it is no good expressing the gift to be
"To my nephew John" since this could apply to either of them.
You should describe the nephew to whom you wish to make
the gift more accurately, either by using his full names, or if his
full names are the same as his cousin, then by words such as
"To my nephew John son of my brother Elijah Bloggins".

A gift to "one of John Bloggins' sons" is void for uncertainty
where John Bloggins has more than one son. A gift which
requires certain people to be selected for the gift but does not
state how or by whom they should be selected is void. Thus, a
gift would be void if it was "to ten soldiers in my unit" or "to
five employees in my company" because it does not state how
the ten soldiers and five employees will be selected.

Purposes
Where a gift is expressed to be for purposes or objects that are uncertain then, probably, it will have no effect because of the uncertainty. Thus where there is a gift of £500 "for cleaning the statue" and there are several statues, then, although a court could hear evidence as to which statue was the most likely to be benefited by the person making the Will, this could lead to great problems and, probably, the gift would not take effect at all. In such a case it is essential to specify, for example, "for cleaning the statue of Queen Victoria in Queens Square, Anytown".

The only situation in which a gift will still take effect, even though it is uncertain, is where the gift is to a charity and there is a general charitable intention. Charities are discussed elsewhere.

The Gift Itself
The item of the gift itself must be obvious and unambiguous. There is no difficulty where it is money because the sum is specified, but where it is property that is being given it must be identifiable. Loose definitions such as "a small portion of what is left" or "some of my best linen" or "a handsome gratuity" are all uncertain and, therefore, there will be no gift.

The safest rule is to remember that there should be no ambiguity. If there is, then you should scrap your Will and re-write it.

Property Which Ceases to be Yours Between the Date of the Will and Death
There can arise the situation where in your Will you make a gift of certain property but dispose of it before your death. If it is some time since you wrote your Will and you have not updated it great complications can arise where property that is given in your Will is later disposed of. The only way in which to prevent this happening is by updating your Will: scrapping the old one and writing a new one when you dispose of any property that is actually mentioned in the Will.

Giving the Same Property Twice
It is carelessness to make more than one gift of the same property, which means that you make a gift of certain property to one person and a gift of the same property to another person.

The property may be shared together between the two persons or, if it can be done, it may be divided up so that each obtains half. You should carefully check your Will to ensure that this situation does not occur.

Where the Will devises or bequeaths property to your husband/wife in absolute terms but also seeks to leave an interest in the same property to your children, obviously there is a conflict. In this situation your husband/wife will take the property absolutely despite the attempted gift of the same property to your children.

Giving More Than You have Got

People often think that their estates are worth far more than they are in reality, and the tendency is to try to give more than you have got. You should have a rough idea of the valuation of your property but then, of course, there will have to be paid Inheritance Tax if you have a large estate; if so you would be sensible to consult a solicitor or an accountant.

You cannot give more than you have got. The effect of trying to do so could be most unfortunate for the recipients of pecuniary legacies, and was fully explained in Chapter 3, page 31.

Check the Value of Your Estate

The way in which to overcome these problems is to sit down when you are considering making a Will and to draw up two lists. In one you should put down all the property that you own, including all the items mentioned in Chapter 3, page 30, with as accurate a valuation against each item as you can manage. With many items this will just be your best estimate or guess. This will give you an idea of how much you are worth. It is then important to make allowance to be deducted from this of all the debts, funeral expenses, bills and Inheritance Tax which will have to be paid out of your estate on your death. In particular, you may have given a financial guarantee to some person which could cause a debt to arise. Your executors might not be aware of the existence of such a guarantee. It is a prudent act to make a clear note of any such guarantee that you have given and to make sure that the note is left either with your Will or in a place where it will be found on your death without difficulty, or to tell your executors during your life of such a guarantee.

You are now in a position to make the other list which is of all the beneficiaries you wish to receive something on your death. These will include the categories given in Chapter 2, page 14 such as relatives, charities and other institutions. You can then put a figure against each beneficiary making sure that you do not exceed in total the value of your estate. It is always best to leave quite a large residue to someone rather than committing your whole estate down to the last penny because it is out of the residue that all the unforeseen debts and Inheritance Tax will have to be paid on your death.

Words

It is important to realise that a Will is interpreted as describing property, people and other matters as at the date of the Will, and not as at the date of the death of the person making the Will.

Words will be given their ordinary dictionary meaning. Where the same words appear in different parts of the Will then it is presumed that they have the same meaning, although much will depend upon the context.

The following are some words which are commonly used in Wills, with an explanation of their meanings and pitfalls.

"beneficiary"   this means someone or something that benefits as a result of a gift in the Will.

"bequeath"   "I bequeath . . ." in a Will usually refers to personal property such as specific items, and money.

"children"   this includes both legitimate and illegitimate children and adopted children if there has been an adoption order. Where a gift is to a child and that child has children and dies before the death of the person making the Will then the gift will pass on to the child or children of that child if they are living at the time of the testator's death unless a contrary intention appears in the Will.

"Children" usually does not include step-children and, if you wish step-children to be included in a gift to "children" then you should specify step-children in addition. "Children" will include step-children where there are only step-children and no other children alive at the date of the making of the Will.

"Children" can also include grand-children where it is clear that this was intended or there are only grandchildren and no other children are alive at the date of making the Will. In order to save confusion you should always specify grandchildren where you wish to have them included.

"descendants"

this means children, grandchildren, great-grandchildren and so on down the line forever. A gift using this word is sometimes phrased as a gift "to my descendants living at my death" which includes all those who are alive at the time of the death of the person making the Will. "Male descendants" means males who are descended from females as well as those who are descended from males. Bear in mind, though, that a gift to "descendants" or "issue" means that all such take in equal shares. If you wish each merely to take in default of a parent or parents (e.g. if a parent predeceases you) then add the words *"per stirpes"*.

"devise"

"I devise . . ." in a Will usually refers to a gift of land (which includes a house).

"executor/executrix" this is the person or persons you appoint to administer your Will and to carry out your wishes as expressed in your Will. Such appointment is done usually by a clause in the Will nominating the executor(s). Anyone can be appointed an executor apart from a minor or a person of unsound mind. A female executor is known as an executrix. A firm of solicitors or an individual solicitor can be appointed but you would do well to ask what fees are charged. Many banks have trustee departments and will act as executors and should be able to tell you their scale of fees. Many people appoint a relative who has some business expertise to be the executor since this saves on fees and, moreover, because it is in the family, it may mean that the Will is administered more cheaply.

There is nothing preventing a person who is an executor also receiving a gift under the Will.

A person who is an executor cannot charge any fees unless this is authorised specifically in your Will. A bank or professional person is unlikely, therefore, to accept the job unless the Will makes provision for these.

An executor can decide whether he wants to do the job or not, and if he decides that he does not, then he can renounce it in writing. You cannot force a person to be executor. For this reason it is best to have two executors. If both declined to act then probate will be granted to the chief beneficiary under the Will.

"family"

this word is to be avoided as it has been defined in several different ways. It means probably no more than "children" but, in order to save confusion, should not be used.

"husband"

this means the husband at the time of making the Will. In the event of a divorce a person remains married until the time of decree absolute (not decree nisi) and up until that time a person can properly be described as a "husband". Divorce means that the Will takes effect unaltered save that any appointment of the former spouse as an executor or trustee is treated as though it were omitted altogether. In addition, any devise or bequest to the former spouse has no effect unless there is a contrary intention expressed in the Will.

In general divorce does not invalidate a Will like a marriage does, but if your marriage splits up it is wise to review the provisions of your Will.

"infant"

this means a child under the age of eighteen. An infant cannot hold a legal estate in land until he reaches eighteen, so land is usually given to trustees until he reaches that age. A pecuniary legacy is often given to a parent or guardian or trustees for the benefit of a person when he reaches eighteen since he cannot give a proper receipt for it until he reaches that age.

"issue"

this means all descendants but has been interpreted as having several

                                different meanings. In a simple Will
                                its use should be avoided.

"minor"   this has the same meaning as
                                "infant".

"nephews"   much will depend upon the context
                                of the Will as to what this means. It
                                is safest to specify their names, or if
                                this is impossible, their relationship
                                with a particular person, such as
                                "the children of my sister Katy".
                                Remember, of course, that "chil-
                                dren" include illegitimate children
                                and so, consequently, "nephews"
                                could also include illegitimates.

"next of kin"   this means the closest blood relation.

"nieces"   the same applies as for "nephew".

"pecuniary legacy"   this is a gift of money in a Will.

"residue"   this means the amount that is left of
                                your estate after effect has been
                                given to all the gifts in your Will and
                                testamentary and other expenses
                                have been paid.

"survivor"   this may apply to persons who are
                                not born at the time of the Will. For
                                example, a gift to "my brothers and
                                sisters who survive me" would
                                include all your brothers and sisters
                                and not just those already born at
                                the time of the Will. Similarly, a gift
                                to "the children of my brother John
                                Bloggins who shall survive me"
                                includes children born to John
                                Bloggins after your death.

"testamentary expenses"   in your Will you may provide for

the residue of your estate to be left to a person or persons after the payment of all "testamentary expenses". This term includes the cost of administering your Will such as executors' expenses, investigations to discover the names and addresses of persons to whom you have left property in your Will, any costs involved in taking legal advice or going to court in order to clarify the meaning of your Will.

"trustee"

a trustee is a person to whom in your Will you give property to be looked after for the benefit of another person. This means that the trustee does not get the benefit of the property but merely holds it on behalf of the person for whom it is intended. If it is a sum of money, for example, the trustee may invest it properly and give the income to the person for whom you intended it in your Will. This is often done in the case of minors. If a sole trustee dies then the estate devolves on his personal representatives but there should always be more than one trustee. Two is a usual number.

As you can see a trustee is someone who is "trusted" with another's property to look after it for that other's benefit. Consequently, if you wish to appoint a trustee you should ask a person whom you feel will deal properly and sensibly with the property. Anyone can be appointed a trustee apart from a minor.

"wife"   this means the wife at the time of making the Will. In the event of a divorce a person remains married until the time of decree absolute (not decree nisi) and up until that time a person can properly be described as a "wife". See also under "husband", page 51.

Where Do I Keep My Will?

Once you have made your Will it should be kept somewhere safe. Moreover, it should be easily available on your death otherwise it might be thought to have been lost.

If your Will cannot be found on your death then it is presumed to have been destroyed by you with the intention that it should no longer be operative. This, of course, would have the most disastrous effect with your property being distributed in a way completely contrary to your intentions and wishes.

Most people prefer to leave their Will deposited at their bank. This means that it is safe, it is easily obtainable on your death and, perhaps most important for many people, no one else is entitled to look at your Will until after your death.

Any Will or codicil may be deposited for safe custody at Somerset House for a fee (see page 157). Somerset House will send you an envelope in which to place your Will. Seal it and complete the information on the outside, giving your name and the details of the executors. Then sign the outside of the sealed envelope in the presence of a witness or a probate registry officer. Keep a photocopy of your Will in case you wish to refer to its contents. Either send the Will in the sealed envelope with a covering letter by registered post to the Record Keeper at Somerset House or take it by hand to any probate registry or sub-registry. You will be given an official certificate that the Will has been deposited and it is important that you should tell your executors that you have done this. You will not be able to withdraw your Will without showing the certificate of deposit (which your executors will have to hand over in the event of your death – so let them know where you keep it). Naturally, no one else is allowed access to your Will. Similar arrangements exist in Northern Ireland.

THE CONTENTS OF THE WILL

1. Statement that this is your last Will and Testament.
2. Your full names and address and the date of the Will.
3. Statement that you revoke all previous Wills made by you.
4. Appointment of executor(s) and payment of executor(s).
5. Appointment of a firm of solicitors to deal with the estate, if you wish, although this is not essential.
6. The method of disposal of your body, such as by cremation or for the purposes of medical science and research and then by cremation. This is not essential.
7. Payment of testamentary expenses.
8. Payment of any Inheritance Tax if you are making gifts "free of tax".
9. Any recital: that is, any statement of affection or moral indebtedness which does not have the effect of making a gift.
10. A list of gifts of specific items.
11. A list of all pecuniary legacies headed "I give and bequeath the following pecuniary legacies".
12. A list of all gifts of land headed "I give and devise . . .".
13. A clause dealing with the residue of your estate: that is, any property or money remaining after all the gifts and payment of expenses in your Will have been made.
14. Your usual signature.
15. The signatures of two witnesses, neither of whom or whose spouses are given any gift in the will. There should be a statement that they were both present at the same time and either saw you making your signature or acknowledging that the signature is yours.

CHECK-LIST OF STEPS TO BE TAKEN

1. Make a list of all your property and property to which you will be entitled in the future. Deduct all your debts, mortgages etc. This will tell you what you can leave in your Will.
2. Make a list of all those persons to whom you want to give something in your Will. These are known as beneficiaries.

3. Note any expressions of affection etc., that you want to make in your Will.

4. Select your executors: members of the family, friends, solicitors or a Bank. Ask them if they are prepared to act as executors. If they are a Bank or professional persons, ask what their fees are, and include in your Will specific provision for these to be paid. If a friend or member of the family, you should make a gift in your Will to them of some reasonable amount for the trouble, unless you are giving them anything else in the Will.

5. Write in a clear hand or, preferably, type your Will using a clean sheet of paper. If you make any mistakes tear up the whole Will and start again. Remember: after your death any alterations may be taken to have been made some time afterwards.

6. Make sure that all the essential parts to the Will, as described "The Contents of the Will", page 55, are included.

7. Make a list of all bequests of your goods that you wish to leave and a list of all the legacies of money that you wish to leave.

8. Consider the question of charities and, if you wish to leave something to a specific charity, make sure that you have the name correct. Also, ask the charity for its suggested legacy clause to insert in your Will. Do you want to express a general charitable intention so that if your gift cannot go to the charity it will go to another?

9. Consider the question of leaving something for your pets.

10. Consider whether you wish to create any trusts. If so, you must appoint trustees and you should obtain their consent beforehand.

11. When you sign your Will make sure that you have two witnesses present who actually see you sign or who acknowledge that it is your signature. Make sure that they then sign the Will themselves. Remember: you cannot leave any gift to your two witnesses, or their husbands/wives.

12. Make sure that your signature is your usual one.

13. Make sure that the Will is dated the day that it is signed.

14. Fold up your Will and place it in an envelope clearly marked "The Last Will and Testament of . . ." and add your name.

15. Put your Will in a safe place where it will not be lost or destroyed. Preferably, take it to your Bank for safe keeping. Keep a photo-copy at home, somewhere safe, but where it will be found on your death.

16. Tell your executors and your next-of-kin where your Will is kept.

17. Do not forget about your Will. From time to time circumstances may change which will make you want to update it. In this case, collect your Will from where it is kept and make a new Will, following the steps outlined above, to take account of the changed circumstances.

18. Once you have made your new Will destroy the old one by tearing it up or burning it. Just crossing it through may not have the effect of making it inoperative.

7

SAMPLE WILLS

Remember:

1. The first two paragraphs of example 1 are necessary in *all Wills*, substituting your own name, and others, and the actual date of the *signing* of the Will in the presence of witnesses.

2. The last paragraph of example 1 starting "As witness . . ." to the end is necessary in *all Wills*, substituting your own usual signature and ensuring that the two witnesses have attested and signed the Will to the effect that they have both witnessed you sign or acknowledged your signature in each other's presence. The witnesses of course, or their husbands or wives, cannot be given anything by the terms of the Will. You should check this.

3. Appointment of executor (called executrix if she is female). You can appoint almost anyone as executor, including someone who is given something by the terms of the Will. You may want to appoint more than one executor so that one is a check upon the other or because you believe a number of heads is better than one. There is

no limit on the number, but do remember that they will all have to get together, so think of them. Usually, two executors are considered sufficient. If it is a simple Will, such as example 1 where everything is left to one person it may be more convenient to appoint that one person as your sole executor.

You should ask a person if he/she is prepared to act as executor before appointing him/her in your Will.

Example 1 shows the appointment of a wife as executrix. Example 2 shows the appointment of a firm of solicitors. You can also appoint a bank, but see the manager first. Do remember that a professional person like a solicitor or a bank official will charge for their services and you must make provision for this in your Will. If you do not, then almost certainly they will decline to act, because they are not entitled to charge fees without specific provision being made for them. A bank will have a scale of fees about which you can ask. These fees and charges will be taken out of your estate. A personal friend or a relative should be entitled to claim expenses for administering your estate, but will not be able to charge for his/her services. This, of course, is a factor to be borne in mind. You may feel, therefore, that in these circumstances a small legacy to each executor would be appropriate to compensate for the time and trouble to which they will be put. It is necessary to appoint an executor so that your Will can be administered.

4.   The same points about executors apply to trustees. Professional ones will charge where a family or friends will not. You should seriously consider having a professional trustee, however, since, in the long view, it may save money. A professional trustee will have far more expertise about investing money in the right places and saving on tax etc. Moreover, some of the law about trustees, what they can and cannot do, is quite complicated.

Remember that you only need trustees where you wish your property to be administered for the benefit of persons or institutions, rather than giving the property outright to those persons or institutions.

5.   The later sample Wills deal with specific situations. You

can adapt them to meet your own requirements. Example 9 deals with £2000 and a pet cat. You could leave any reasonable amount of money you care to and in favour of any pet animal such as a dog, horse, hamster or whatever. Likewise, you can adapt the other examples.

6. There may be several of the examples, or adaptations to them, which meet your requirements. You can include all these in your one Will, provided there is the property to meet the claims, of course! You can be as detailed as you wish in your Will about your property. However, remember that if, before you die, you dispose of any specific item bequeathed by your Will, then the person to whom it was given is not entitled to any other item in substitution. It is wise, therefore, not to bequeath under your Will specific items you are likely to dispose of before you die. You can include any number of different methods of disposing of your property so long as the essentials mentioned in paragraphs 1, 2 and 3 are included in the Will.

7. In most cases, once you have made specific gifts of property or money, there still remains the rest of your estate. This is known as the residue. You should always make provision for the residue to go to someone or to some institution otherwise it may turn out that you have not disposed of all your property in your Will.

Statutory Will Forms

This term does *not* refer to the forms you can get from stationers on which you can write your Will.

In order to save writing out at length certain matters in your Will these Statutory Will Forms can be incorporated into your Will by you stating in your Will that you want them to be incorporated.

Some of the more useful ones are included below:

Form 1

It may be that during your lifetime you agree to give property to a certain person. Let us say you agree to give Mr. Bloggins £500. Perhaps you wish to leave Mr. Bloggins an additional £500 in your Will and you insert in your Will a clause to that effect. However, if the first £500 has not been paid by the date of your death, or even if it has, in certain circumstances, the £500 left to him in your Will is taken as being in satisfaction of the agreement to give him the first £500.

This means that Mr. Bloggins will receive only £500 although you intended to give him £1000! The only way in which to clarify this is to insert a clause in your Will that states that any gift under your Will is in addition to any other gift. This is done by adopting Form 1 which states:

"I confirm every settlement of property made by me which is subsisting at my death, and subject to any express provision to the contrary in my Will, the provisions made by my Will for the benefit of persons beneficially interested under any such settlement, shall be in addition to, and not in satisfaction of, those made, or covenanted to be made by me in such settlement."

Form 1 can be adopted in your Will by inserting the clause "Form 1 of the Statutory Will Forms, 1925, is incorporated in this my Will".

Form 2

If you wished to leave someone all your personal effects including those set out in Statutory Will Forms, 1925, Form 2 (see below) then there would be no need to write out all these items. All you need to do is insert in your Will the clause "Form 2 of the Statutory Will Forms, 1925, is incorporated in this my Will". You can then leave "personal chattels" to the person you wish without having to specify all the items since "personal chattels" will be taken to include everything mentioned in Form 2. You can still use Form 2 if you do not possess some of the items mentioned in Form 2: using this form merely includes any such items as are mentioned which you do have and are able to dispose of.

A similar thing to Form 2 is the list set out in S.55(1)(X) of the Administration of Estates Act, 1925 and, if you prefer, you can quote this section rather than referring to Form 2. The difference is that Form 2 specifically includes wearing apparel. S.55(1)(X) does not.

Remember that S.55(1)(X) and Form 2 are only there to be used if you wish to. You do not have to use them. Instead you may wish to write out a list of all your personal effects. If you wish to leave some personal effects to one person and some to another then, of course, you cannot use S.55(1)(X) or Form 2 and, instead, you must specify which personal items you wish to leave to which person.

Form 2 states:
1. "'Personal Chattels' shall mean 'carriages, horses, stable furniture and effects (not used for business purposes), motor cars and accessories (not used for business purposes), garden effects, domestic animals, plate, plated articles, linen, china, glass, books, pictures, prints, furniture, jewellery, articles of household or personal use or ornament (including wearing apparel), also musical and scientific instruments and apparatus, wines, liquors and consumable stores, but shall not include any chattels, used at my death for business purposes, nor money or securities for money.
2. But a general disposition of personal chattels shall take effect subject to any specific disposition."

   S.55(1)(X) of the Administration of Estates Act, 1925 reads: "Personal Chattels" means carriages, horses, stable furniture and effects (not used for business purposes), motor cars and accessories (not used for business purposes), garden effects, domestic animals, plate, plated articles, linen, china, glass, books, pictures, prints, furniture, jewellery, articles of household or personal use or ornament, musical and scientific instruments and apparatus, wines, liquors and consumable stores, but do not include any chattels used at the death . . . for business purposes nor money nor securities for money.

Form 4
This clarifies the situation of gifts being left to charities. As we know, a money gift is known as a legacy. Form 4 directs that the responsibility of those who deal with your estate after your death for seeing that a legacy to a charity is actually paid is discharged if the legacy is given to the charity's treasurer or other officer of the charity. In other words, it makes life easier for those who have to pay the legacies to charity out of your estate after your death. However, as mentioned previously, it is safer to obtain from the charity concerned its own recommended form of legacy clause. This has the added advantage of ensuring you name the charity correctly!

List of Sample Wills

1. A married man with or without children wishing to leave everything to his wife.

2. A married man wishing to leave everything to his wife who is suffering from mental disability.

3. A married man with two children wishing to leave his wife a life interest in his property and, upon her death or remarriage, everything to his children.

4. A married man with six children wishing to make various dispositions and leaving the house and contents and residue to his wife.

5. A married man with a wife and children who wishes to leave his house and its contents to his wife for her life but free of the mortgage. He wishes the rest of his estate, whether it be land or other property, to be sold and converted into money so that it can be invested. He wishes to give his wife an income for the rest of her life from the rest of his estate and, on her death, the whole of his estate, including the house and contents, to go to his two children equally.

6. A married man with two children wishing to leave his wife one half of his estate together with a life interest in the other half; upon her death the half in which she had a life interest to go to the two children.

7. A married man with two children wishing to leave his wife one half of his estate and his two children the other half.

8. A person wishing to leave all his personal effects to another person.

9. A person who wishes to leave a sum of money for the maintenance of his/her pet cat. The residue of the estate to go to a home for sick animals.

10. A person who wishes to leave everything to his/her son who is under the age of eighteen (that is a minor). A provision is included for the property to go to charity if the son dies before he reaches 25 or during the person's lifetime.

11. A single person wishing to leave everything to be shared equally between his brothers and sisters living at the date of the Will.

12. A single person wishing to leave everything to be shared between his brother and sister.

13. A single person wishing to leave everything to be shared equally between his brothers and sisters, including those not yet born.

14. A person wishing to leave a sum of money to charities to be selected by his/her trustees.

15. A widow wishing to leave everything to her two children who are over the age of eighteen in equal shares.

16. A widow with two daughters (one married with a son and one unmarried) wishing to leave everything to the unmarried daughter but noting affection for the married daughter. A provision is added that everything should go to her grandson if the unmarried daughter should die before her.

17. A man married for the second time who wishes to give legacies of £500 to each of his wife's children by her first marriage (i.e. his step-children). If they should die beforehand then the money should go to their own children. If they have no children then the money should become part of the residue of the estate.

18. A person wishing to leave land, specific items and also pecuniary legacies to certain persons.

19. A person wishing to dispose of his business to his son.

20. A person wishing to leave everything to his wife and his body for spare-part surgery or for medical research or education.

21. A person wishing to have his property disposed of according to the law of intestacy (as set out in Chapter 8, "Who Benefits If I Make No Will?") but wanting to revoke all previous Wills.

1) *A married man with or without children wishing to leave everything to his wife.*

This is the last Will and Testament of me Arthur Bruce Bloggins of 1 Whiteacre, Blacktown in the county of Greenshire, made this . . . day of . . ., one thousand nine hundred and . . .

I hereby revoke all former Wills made by me and declare this to be my last Will.

I appoint my wife Ann Belinda Bloggins to be the sole executrix of this my Will.

I devise and bequeath all my real and personal estate whatsoever and wheresoever to my wife Ann Belinda Bloggins absolutely if she shall survive me by 30 days.

If she shall not survive me by 30 days then I devise and bequeath all my real and personal estate whatsoever and wheresoever to be divided equally among such of my children as shall be living at the date of my death.

As Witness my hand the day and year first above written.

Signed by the said testator in the presence of us, present at the same time, who at his request and in his presence have subscribed our names as witnesses.

Arthur B. Bloggins

Adam Smith

of 2 The Cottages,
Blacktown
(Bricklayer)

Milton Freeman

of 3 Smallacre,
Blacktown
(Motor Mechanic)

NOTE: If the testator has no children then, to cover the possibility of his wife not surviving him by 30 days he should make provision for his estate to go elsewhere, for example to a charity.

The reason the gift to his wife is conditional on his wife surviving him by 30 days is to prevent the situation where, say, both are involved in a car crash and his wife dies a few days after him. If there was no condition that she has to survive him by 30 days then, on his death, his property would pass to his wife but on her death, a few days later, the property would pass according to her Will or, if she had not made a Will, to her relations and not as the testator would have wished it.

2) A married man wishing to leave everything to his wife who is suffering from mental disability.

This is the last Will and Testament of me Arthur Bruce Bloggins of 1 Whiteacre, Blacktown in the county of Greenshire, made this . . . day of . . ., one thousand nine hundred and . . .

I hereby revoke all former Wills made by me and declare this to be my last Will.

I appoint Messrs. Smith, Jones and Browne of Peradventure Passage, Blacktown (hereinafter called my trustees, which expression shall include the trustees for the time being hereof) to be the executors and trustees of this my Will. My trustees shall be entitled to charge and be paid out of the residue of my estate all professional or other charges for all business or acts done by them in connection with this my Will.

I devise and bequeath all my real and personal estate whatsoever and wheresoever to my trustees upon trust to pay my funeral and testamentary expenses and to stand possessed of the residue during the lifetime of my wife Ann Belinda Bloggins and to receive the income thereof and apply the same as they shall in their absolute discretion determine for the maintenance or benefit of my said wife if she shall survive me by 30 days.

Notwithstanding anything herein expressed my trustees may in their absolute discretion at any time pay for the maintenance or benefit of my said wife any part or parts of the capital of the said residue even though such parts may amount in aggregate to the whole thereof.

After her death, I direct my trustees to apply my said estate to the Save Our Souls Society or other charitable uses as they in their absolute discretion shall think fit. I declare that the receipt of the person professing to be the treasurer or other duly authorised officer of the said Society shall be deemed a full and sufficient discharge to my trustees who shall not be bound to see to the application thereof.

As Witness my hand the day and year first above written.

Signed by the said testator in the
presence of us, present at the
same time, who at his request
and in his presence have
subscribed our names as
witnesses.

Arthur B. Bloggins

Adam Smith

of 2 The Cottages,
Blacktown
(Bricklayer)

Milton Freeman

of 3 Smallacre,
Blacktown
(Motor Mechanic)

3) A married man with two children wishing to leave his wife a life interest in his property and, upon her death or remarriage, everything to his children.

This is the last Will and Testament of me Arthur Bruce Bloggins of 1 Whiteacre, Blacktown in the County of Greenshire, made this . . . day of . . ., one thousand nine hundred and . . .

I hereby revoke all former Wills made by me and declare this to be my last Will.

I appoint Messrs. Smith, Jones and Browne of Peradventure Passage, Blacktown (hereinafter called my trustees, which expression shall include the trustees for the time being hereof) to be the executors and trustees of this my Will. My trustees shall be entitled to charge and be paid out of the residue of my estate all professional or other charges for all business or acts done by them in connection with this my Will.

I devise and bequeath all my real and personal estate whatsoever and wheresoever to my trustees upon trust to sell the same with power to postpone sale and to invest the proceeds thereof and to apply the income therefrom for the benefit of my wife Ann Belinda Bloggins until she dies or remarries, whichever is the sooner, and thereafter to divide the said proceeds amongst those of my children as shall be living at the date of my wife's death or remarriage, whichever is the sooner, in equal parts absolutely.

Notwithstanding anything herein expressed my trustees may in their absolute discretion at any time pay for the maintenance or benefit of my said wife any part or parts of the capital of the residue even though such parts may amount in the aggregate to the whole thereof.

As Witness my hand the day and year first above written.

Signed by the said testator in the presence of us, present at the same time, who at his request and in his presence have subscribed our names as witnesses.

Arthur B. Bloggins

Adam Smith

of 2 The Cottages,
Blacktown
(Bricklayer)

Milton Freeman

of 3 Smallacre,
Blacktown
(Motor Mechanic)

*NOTE: Depending on age and circumstances, many spouses
would not wish to apply the restrictive clause about
remarriage in full or at all. Protection against gold-digging
prospective spouses and of "family" capital may require
consideration.*

4) *A married man with six children wishing to make various dispositions and leaving the house and contents and residue to his wife.*

This is the last Will and Testament of me Arthur Bruce Bloggins of 1 Whiteacre, Blacktown in the County of Greenshire, made this . . . day of . . ., one thousand nine hundred and . . .

I hereby revoke all former Wills made by me and declare this to be my last Will.

I appoint my wife Ann Belinda Bloggins and my son Percy Bloggins to be the executors of this my Will.

I devise and bequeath my freehold land and property at 1, Whiteacre, Blacktown, aforesaid, or if this should be sold or otherwise disposed of during my lifetime, any other house owned by me that is my residence at the date of my death, freed and discharged from all sums secured thereon by way of mortgage or otherwise at my death, together with my furniture and effects of household use and ornament therein which my executors in their absolute discretion consider belonging thereto (save such of the same as may be otherwise specifically disposed of by this my Will) to my wife Ann Belinda Bloggins absolutely, if she shall survive me by 30 days, or, if she shall not survive me by 30 days or if she shall predecease me, to be sold and the proceeds divided equally between those of my children living at the date of my death.

I direct that such sums and all interest and other costs and expenses incurred in respect of the discharge of any said mortgage or other encumbrance shall be paid out of the residue of my estate.

I give and bequeath my Ford Escort motor car or, if this should be sold or otherwise disposed of during my lifetime, any other motor car owned by me at the date of my death to my son Charles Bloggins.

I give and bequeath my stamp collection to my son Arthur Bloggins.

I give and bequeath the following pecuniary legacies subject to tax:

1. To my daughter Amanda Bloggins the sum of one thousand pounds (£1000).
2. To my son Charles Bloggins the sum of five hundred pounds (£500).
3. To my daughter Elizabeth Smithers the sum of five hundred pounds (£500).
4. To my son Arthur Bloggins the sum of five hundred pounds (£500).
5. To my son Percy Bloggins the sum of one thousand, five hundred pounds (£1500).
6. To my daughter Suzannah Bloggins the sum of eight hundred pounds (£800).

I devise and bequeath the residue of my real and personal estate whatsoever and wheresoever to my wife Ann Belinda Bloggins absolutely if she shall survive me by 30 days or, if she shall not survive me by 30 days, to be divided equally between those of my children living at the date of my death.

As Witness my hand the day and year first above written.

Signed by the said testator in the presence of us, present at the same time, who at his request and in his presence have subscribed our names as witnesses.

Arthur B. Bloggins

Adam Smith

of 2 The Cottages,
Blacktown
(Bricklayer)

Milton Freeman

of 3 Smallacre,
Blacktown
(Motor Mechanic)

Continued overleaf

Continued from previous page

NOTE: *This Sample Will assumes that all the children will be over the age of eighteen at the date of the testator's death. If there is a danger that some might not be then their gifts will have to be held in trust until they reach the age of eighteen. See Sample Will No. 10.*

5) *A married man with a wife and children who wishes to leave his house and its contents to his wife for her life but free of the mortgage. He wishes the rest of his estate, whether it be land or other property to be sold and converted into money so that it can be invested. He wishes to give his wife an income for the rest of her life from the rest of his estate, and, on her death or re-marriage, the whole of his estate including the house and contents to go to his two children equally.*

This is the last Will and Testament of me Arthur Bruce Bloggins of 1, Whiteacre, Blacktown in the County of Greenshire, made this . . . day of . . ., one thousand nine hundred and . . .

I hereby revoke all former Wills made by me and declare this to be my last Will.

I appoint Messrs. Smith, Jones and Browne of Peradventure Passage, Blacktown (hereinafter called my trustees, which expression shall include the trustees for the time being thereof) to be the executors and trustees of this my Will. My trustees shall be entitled to charge and be paid out of the residue of my estate all professional or other charges for all business or acts done by them in connection with this my Will.

I devise and bequeath my freehold land and property of 1, Whiteacre, Blacktown, aforesaid or, if this should be sold or otherwise disposed of during my lifetime, any other house owned by me that is my residence at the date of my death, freed and discharged from all sums secured thereon by way of mortgage or otherwise at my death to my trustees upon trust for my wife Ann Belinda Bloggins during her life or until she remarries; and after her death or remarriage, whichever is the sooner, upon trust to such of my children as are living at the date of her death or remarriage, whichever is the sooner, in equal parts absolutely.

I direct that such sums and all interest and other costs and expenses incurred in respect of the discharge of any said mortgage or other encumbrance shall be paid out of the residue of my estate.

Continued overleaf

Continued from previous page

I direct that my trustees shall have the power in agreement with my wife, Ann Belinda Bloggins, to sell any such residence aforesaid and to purchase another with the proceeds or part of the proceeds of sale thereof.

I give all my furniture and effects of household use and ornament which my executors in their absolute discretion consider belonging to my residence (save such of the same as may be otherwise specifically disposed of by this Will) to my wife Ann Belinda Bloggins absolutely.

(At this point you should set out any gifts you may wish to give to other people or institutions.)

I devise and bequeath the residue of my real and personal estate to my trustees upon trust to sell the same and to hold the net proceeds of sale and invest the same and to apply the income therefrom for the benefit of my wife Ann Belinda Bloggins during her life or until she remarries, and after her death or remarriage, whichever is the sooner, upon trust to such of my children as are living at the date of my death in equal parts absolutely.

Notwithstanding anything herein expressed, my trustees may in their absolute discretion at any time pay for the maintenance or benefit of my said wife any part or parts of the capital of the said residue even though such parts may amount in aggregate to the whole thereof.

As Witness my hand the day and year first above written.

Signed by the said testator in the
presence of us, present at the
same time, who at his request
and in his presence have
subscribed our names as
witnesses.

Arthur B. Bloggins

Adam Smith

of 2 The Cottages,
Blacktown
(Bricklayer)

Milton Freeman

of 3 Smallacre,
Blacktown
(Motor Mechanic)

Note: See note on page 69.

6) *A married man with two children wishing to leave his wife one half of his estate together with a life interest in the other half; upon her death the half in which she had a life interest to go to the two children.*

This is the last Will and Testament of me Arthur Bruce Bloggins of 1, Whiteacre, Blacktown in the County of Greenshire, made this . . . day of . . ., one thousand nine hundred and . . .

I hereby revoke all former Wills made by me and declare this to be my last Will.

I appoint Messrs. Smith, Jones and Browne of Peradventure Passage, Blacktown (hereinafter called my trustees, which expression shall include the trustees for the time being hereof) to be the executors and trustees of this my Will. My trustees shall be entitled to charge and be paid out of the residue of my estate all professional or other charges for all business or acts done by them in connection with this my Will.

I devise all my real and personal estate whatsoever and wheresoever to my trustees upon trust to sell the same and to apply the proceeds of sale thereof, but with power to postpone the sale, as follows:

1. To my wife Ann Belinda Bloggins one half of the net proceeds of sale thereof absolutely if she shall survive me by 30 days.
2. To my wife Ann Belinda Bloggins the income from the other half of the net proceeds of sale thereof until she dies or remarries, whichever is the sooner, and, thereafter, to my two children Charles Alan Bloggins and Susan Rachel Bloggins in equal parts absolutely.

If she shall not survive me by 30 days then her half of the net proceeds of sale shall be applied in the same way as the other half of the net proceeds of sale.

Provided that if one or other of my two said children shall die before he/she becomes entitled then his/her share shall vest in the other said child absolutely.

As Witness my hand the day and year first above written.

Signed by the said testator in the
presence of us, present at the
same time, who at his request
and in his presence have
subscribed our names as
witnesses.

Arthur B. Bloggins

Adam Smith

of 2 The Cottages,
Blacktown
(Bricklayer)

Milton Freeman

of 3 Smallacre,
Blacktown
(Motor Mechanic)   *Note: See note on page 69.*

*NOTE: This means that if Charles or Susan dies before he/she
    becomes entitled to receive his/her share (that is, before the
    death of their mother Ann Belinda Bloggins) then the share
    of the child who has died will go to the other child.*

*   If you wished his/her share to go not to the other child,
but to the dead child's children then the clause should read:*

**"Provided that if one or other of my two said children shall
die before he/she becomes entitled then his/her share shall
descend to his/her children living at the date of his/her
death, if any, and if more than one in equal shares, and, in
default of there being any such children, his/her share shall
vest in my other said child absolutely."**

7) *A married man with two children wishing to leave his wife one half of his estate and his two children the other half.*

This is the last Will and Testament of me Arthur Bruce Bloggins of 1, Whiteacre, Blacktown in the County of Greenshire, made this . . . day of . . ., one thousand nine hundred and . . .

I hereby revoke all former Wills made by me and declare this to be my last Will.

I appoint my wife Ann Belinda Bloggins and my son Charles Alan Bloggins to be the executors of this my Will.

I devise and bequeath half my real and personal estate whatsoever and wheresoever to my wife Ann Belinda Bloggins absolutely if she shall survive me by 30 days and the other half of my real and personal estate whatsoever and wheresoever to my son Charles Alan Bloggins and to my daughter Susan Rachel Bloggins in equal parts absolutely.

If my wife shall not survive me by 30 days or if either my wife or my two children or one of them shall predecease me then his/her share shall accrue to my estate and be divided amongst my wife and two children, or those remaining, in equal parts absolutely.

As Witness my hand the day and year first above written.

Signed by the said testator in the
presence of us, present at the
same time, who at his request
and in his presence have
subscribed our names as
witnesses.

Arthur B. Bloggins

Adam Smith

of 2 The Cottages,
Blacktown
(Bricklayer)

Milton Freeman

of 3 Smallacre,
Blacktown
(Motor Mechanic)

8) *A person wishing to leave all his personal effects to another person.*

This is the last Will and Testament of me Arthur Bruce Bloggins of 1, Whiteacre, Blacktown in the County of Greenshire, made this . . . day of . . ., one thousand nine hundred and . . .

I hereby revoke all former Wills made by me and declare this to be my last Will.

I appoint Messrs. Jones, Smith and Browne of Peradventure Passage, Blacktown (hereinafter called my trustees, which expression shall include the trustees for the time being thereof) to be the executors and trustees of this my Will. My trustees shall be entitled to charge and be paid out of the residue of my estate all professional or other charges for all business or acts done by them in connection with this my Will.

Form 2 of the Statutory Wills Forms, 1925, is incorporated in this my Will.

I give and bequeath to Alan Brian Smith of the Whitehouse, Red Lane, Blacktown in the County of Greenshire absolutely and free of tax all my personal chattels.

(At this point you should set out any gifts you may wish to give to other people or institutions and make provision for the residue of your estate.)

As Witness my hand the day and year first above written.

Signed by the said testator in the
presence of us, present at the
same time, who at his request
and in his presence have
subscribed our names as
witnesses.

Arthur B. Bloggins

John Galbreth

of 3 The Cottages,
Blacktown
(Travel Agent)

Milton Freeman

of 3 Smallacre,
Blacktown
(Motor Mechanic)

9) *A person who wishes to leave a sum of money for the maintenance of his/her pet cat. The residue of the estate to go to a home for sick animals.*

This is the last Will and Testament of me Rachel Myfanwy Bloggins of 1, Whiteacre, Blacktown in the County of Greenshire, made this . . . day of . . ., one thousand nine hundred and . . .

I hereby revoke all former Wills made by me and declare this to be my last Will.

I appoint Messrs. Smith, Jones and Browne of Peradventure Passage, Blacktown (hereinafter called my trustees, which expression shall include the trustees for the time being thereof) to be the executors and trustees of this my Will. My trustees shall be entitled to charge and be paid out of the residue of my estate all professional or other charges for all business or acts done by them in connection with this my Will.

I bequeath to my trustees the sum of £2,000 upon trust to invest the same and to apply the income therefrom for the maintenance of my pet tabby cat called Samantha for the period of twenty-one years from the date of my death if my cat shall so long live. After the death of my cat or after the expiration of the period of twenty-one years whichever is the sooner the sum of £2,000 (or the investments then representing the same), shall become part of the residue of my estate.

(At this point you should set out any gifts you may wish to give to other people or institutions.)

I devise and bequeath the residue of all my real and personal estate whatsoever and wheresoever to the Bloggins' Memorial Society for Sick Animals, Blacktown, or to such other charity as my trustees shall in their absolute discretion decide. I declare that the receipt of the person professing to be the treasurer or other duly authorised officer of the said Society shall be deemed a full and sufficient discharge to my trustees who shall not be bound to see to the application thereof.

As Witness my hand the day and year first above written.

Signed by the said testatrix in
the presence of us, present at the
same time, who at her request
and in her presence have
subscribed our names as
witnesses.

R. Myfanwy Bloggins

Adam Smith

of 2 The Cottages,
Blacktown
(Bricklayer)

Milton Freeman

of 3 Smallacre,
Blacktown
(Motor Mechanic)

10) *A person who wishes to leave everything to his/her son who is under the age of eighteen (that is a minor). A provision is included for the property to go to charity if the son dies before he reaches 25 or during the person's lifetime.*

This is the last Will and Testament of me Arthur Bruce Bloggins of 1, Whiteacre, Blacktown in the County of Greenshire, made this . . . day of . . ., one thousand nine hundred and . . .

I hereby revoke all former Wills made by me and declare this to be my last Will.

I appoint Messrs. Smith, Jones and Browne of Peradventure Passage, Blacktown (hereinafter called my trustees, which expression shall include the trustees for the time being thereof) to be the executors and trustees of this my Will. My trustees shall be entitled to charge and be paid out of the residue of my estate all professional or other charges for all business or acts done by them in connection with this my Will.

I devise and bequeath all my real and personal estate whatsoever and wheresoever to my trustees upon trust to pay my funeral and testamentary expenses and to stand possessed of the residue and to apply the capital and income therefrom for the benefit of my son Jason Bloggins until he reaches the age of twenty-five and, thereafter, to him absolutely.

Provided that, if my said son shall die after my death under the age of twenty-five or in my lifetime then I devise and bequeath all my real and personal estate aforesaid to the charity the Save Our Souls Society. I declare that the receipt of the person professing to be the treasurer or other duly authorised officer of the said Society shall be deemed a full and sufficient discharge to my trustees who shall not be bound to see to the application thereof.

For the avoidance of doubt I desire that all my real and personal estate aforesaid shall be applied for charitable purposes in the event of my son's prior death as provided.

As Witness my hand the day and year first above written.

Signed by the said testator in the
presence of us, present at the
same time, who at his request   *Arthur B. Bloggins*
and in his presence have
subscribed our names as
witnesses.

Adam Smith

of 2 The Cottages,
Blacktown
(Bricklayer)

Milton Freeman

of 3 Smallacre,
Blacktown
(Motor Mechanic)

*NOTE: Under the terms of this Will all the estate will go to the
charity if the son dies under the age of twenty-five or during
the testator's lifetime even if the son was married and had
issue. If the person wishes to leave all or any of the estate in
this event to the son's wife or issue then he should state this.
Not specifying any charity or beneficiary in the event of the
son's predecease or death before the age of 25 would have
the effect of all the estate going to the son's issue, if any.*

11) A single person wishing to leave everything to be shared equally between his brothers and sisters living at the date of the Will.

This is the last Will and Testament of me Arthur Bruce Bloggins of 1, Whiteacre, Blacktown in the County of Greenshire, made this . . . day of . . ., one thousand nine hundred and . . .

I hereby revoke all former Wills made by me and declare this to be my last Will.

I appoint my sister Pamela Bloggins and my brother Paul Bloggins to be the executors of this my Will.

I devise and bequeath all my real and personal estate whatsoever and wheresoever to all my brothers and sisters of the whole blood living at the date of this my Will in equal shares absolutely, and, in the event of any of my brothers and sisters of the whole blood pre-deceasing me I direct that the children of any of those who pre-decease me shall take that share in equal parts absolutely.

As Witness my hand the day and year first above written.

Signed by the said testator in the
presence of us, present at the
same time, who at his request
and in his presence have
subscribed our names as
witnesses.

Arthur B. Bloggins

Adam Smith

of 2 The Cottages,
Blacktown
(Bricklayer)

Milton Freeman

of 3 Smallacre,
Blacktown
(Motor Mechanic)

*NOTE: Specifying brothers and sisters "of the whole blood"
excludes half-brothers and half-sisters and step-brothers
and step-sisters. If you wish to include these you should
delete "of the whole blood" and specifically include half-
brothers and half-sisters and step-brothers and step-sisters.*

*12) A single person wishing to leave everything to be shared
    between his brother and sister.*

This is the last Will and Testament of me Arthur Bruce
Bloggins of 1, Whiteacre, Blacktown in the County of
Greenshire, made this . . . day of . . ., one thousand nine
hundred and . . .

I hereby revoke all former Wills made by me and declare
this to be my last Will.

I appoint my brother Paul Bloggins and my sister Pamela
Bloggins to be the executors of this my Will.

I devise and bequeath all my real and personal estate
whatsoever and wheresoever to my brother Paul Bloggins
and my sister Pamela Bloggins in equal shares absolutely,
provided that, if either pre-decease me, his or her children,
if any, shall take that share in equal parts absolutely.

As Witness my hand the day and year first above written.

Signed by the said testator in the
presence of us, present at the
same time, who at his request
and in his presence have
subscribed our names as
witnesses.

Arthur B. Bloggins

Adam Smith

of 2 The Cottages,
Blacktown
(Bricklayer)

Milton Freeman

of 3 Smallacre,
Blacktown
(Motor Mechanic)

13) *A single person wishing to leave everything to be shared equally between his brothers and sisters, including those not yet born.*

This is the last Will and Testament of me Arthur Bruce Bloggins of 1, Whiteacre, Blacktown in the County of Greenshire, made this . . . day of . . ., one thousand nine hundred and . . .

I hereby revoke all former Wills made by me and declare this to be my last Will.

I appoint Messrs. Smith, Jones and Browne of Peradventure Passage, Blacktown (hereinafter called my trustees, which expression shall include the trustees for the time being thereof) to be the executors and trustees of this my Will. My trustees shall be entitled to charge and be paid out of the residue of my estate all professional or other charges for all business or acts done by them in connection with this my Will.

I devise and bequeath all my real and personal estate whatsoever and wheresoever to all my brothers and sisters of the whole blood in equal shares absolutely, and, in the event of any of my brothers and sisters of the whole blood pre-deceasing me, I direct that the children of any of those who pre-decease me shall take that share in equal parts absolutely.

As Witness my hand the day and year first above written.

Signed by the said testator in the
presence of us, present at the
same time, who at his request
and in his presence have
subscribed our names as
witnesses.

Arthur B. Bloggins

Adam Smith

of 2 The Cottages,
Blacktown
(Bricklayer)

Milton Freeman

of 3 Smallacre,
Blacktown
(Motor Mechanic)

*NOTE: Specifying brothers and sisters "of the whole blood"
excludes half-brothers and half-sisters and step-brothers
and step-sisters. If you wish to include these you should
delete "of the whole blood" and specifically include half-
brothers and half-sisters and step-brothers and step-sisters.*

*This form of Will is to be discouraged as the estate cannot be
distributed until such time as there is no chance of any further
brothers or sisters being born. This will be only when the
testator's mother is beyond child-bearing age which could be
a long time in the future.*

14) *A person wishing to leave a sum of money to charities to be
    selected by his/her trustees.*

This is the last Will and Testament of me Arthur Bruce
Bloggins of 1, Whiteacre, Blacktown in the County of
Greenshire, made this . . . day of . . ., one thousand nine
hundred and . . .

I hereby revoke all former Wills made by me and declare
this to be my last Will.

I appoint Messrs. Smith, Jones and Browne of Peradventure
Passage, Blacktown (hereinafter called my trustees, which
expression shall include the trustees for the time being
thereof) to be the executors and trustees of this my Will.
My trustees shall be entitled to charge and be paid out of
the residue of my estate, all professional or other charges
for all business or acts done by them in connection with this
my Will.

I bequeath to my trustees the sum of £500 upon trust to
apply the same for such charitable objects or institutions
as my trustees in their absolute discretion may select.

*(At this point you should set out any other gifts you may
wish to give to other people or institutions and make
provisions for the residue of your estate.)*

As Witness my hand the day and year first above written.

Signed by the said testator in the
presence of us, present at the
same time, who at his request
and in his presence have
subscribed our names as
witnesses.

Arthur B. Bloggins

Adam Smith

of 2 The Cottages,
Blacktown
(Bricklayer)

Milton Freeman

of 3 Smallacre,
Blacktown
(Motor Mechanic)

15) *A widow wishing to leave everything to her two children who are over the age of eighteen in equal shares.*

This is the last Will and Testament of me Ann Belinda Bloggins of 1, Whiteacre, Blacktown in the County of Greenshire made this . . . day of . . ., one thousand nine hundred and . . .

I hereby revoke all former Wills made by me and declare this to be my last Will.

I appoint my son Charles Alan Bloggins of 1, Whiteacre, Blacktown, aforesaid and my daughter Susan Rachel Bloggins of 2, White Cottages, Blacktown aforesaid to be the executors of this my Will.

I devise and bequeath all my real and personal estate whatsoever and wheresoever to my son Charles Alan Bloggins and my daughter Susan Rachel Bloggins in equal shares absolutely, provided that, if either pre-decease me, his or her children, if any, shall take that share in equal parts absolutely.

As Witness my hand the day and year first above written.

**Signed by the said testatrix
in the presence of us,
present at the same time,
who at her request and in
her presence have
subscribed our names as
witnesses.**

A B Bloggins

Adam Smith

**of 2 The Cottages,
Blacktown
(Bricklayer)**

Milton Freeman

**of 3 Smallacre,
Blacktown
(Motor Mechanic)**

16) A widow with two daughters (one married with a son and one unmarried) wishing to leave everything to the unmarried daughter but noting affection for the married daughter. A provision is added that everything should go to her grandson if the unmarried daughter should die before her.

This is the last Will and Testament of me Ann Belinda Bloggins of 1, Whiteacre, Blacktown in the County of Greenshire made this . . . day of . . ., one thousand nine hundred and . . .

I hereby revoke all former Wills made by me and declare this to be my last Will.

I appoint my daughter Susan Rachel Bloggins of 2, White Cottages, Blacktown, to be the sole executrix of this my Will provided she shall survive me for 30 days.

Whereas I hold my daughter Elizabeth Jane Smithers in great affection I believe and recognise that she is well provided for by her husband Peter George Smithers.

Therefore I devise and bequeath all my real and personal estate whatsoever and wheresoever to my daughter Susan Rachel Bloggins absolutely.

Provided that if my daughter Susan Rachel Bloggins should not survive me by 30 days then I appoint my daughter Elizabeth Jane Smithers and her husband Peter George Smithers to be the executors of this my Will and I devise and bequeath all my real and personal estate to my grandson Jason Caleb Smithers absolutely.

As Witness my hand the day and year first above written.

Signed by the said testatrix in
the presence of us, present at the
same time, who at her request
and in her presence have
subscribed our names as
witnesses.

A B Bloggins

Adam Smith

of 2 The Cottages,
Blacktown
(Bricklayer)

Milton Freeman

of 3 Smallacre,
Blacktown
(Motor Mechanic)

*This Will presumes that Jason is over 18, otherwise it
would require clauses similar to Sample Will 10 (Page 84).
Ann Bloggins must remember that the Will would need alteration if
any changes occurred in the financial circumstances of Elizabeth
Jane, or there were more children.*

17) A man married for the second time who wishes to leave legacies of £500 to each of his wife's children by her first marriage (i.e. his step-children). If they should die beforehand then the money should go to their own children. If they have no children then the money should become part of the residue of the estate.

This is the last Will and Testament of me Arthur Bruce Bloggins of 1, Whiteacre, Blacktown in the County of Greenshire, made this . . . day of . . ., one thousand nine hundred and . . .

I hereby revoke all former Wills made by me and declare this to be my last Will.

I appoint my wife Ann Belinda Bloggins of 1, Whiteacre, Blacktown aforesaid, to be my sole executrix of this my Will.

I give and bequeath the following pecuniary legacies subject to tax:

1. To my stepson Charles Smithers the sum of five hundred pounds (£500).
2. To my stepdaughter Susan Smithers the sum of five hundred pounds (£500).

Provided that if one or the other of them shall die before me then his or her legacy, as the case may be, shall be shared equally among his or her children, and not the children of the other stepchild, living at the date of my death. In default of there being any children of the stepchild who will have predeceased me then the said legacy shall become part of the residue of my estate.

I devise and bequeath the residue of all my real and personal estate whatsoever and wheresoever to my wife Ann Belinda Bloggins absolutely if she shall survive me by 30 days.

If she shall not survive me by 30 days the residue of my estate is to be divided equally between my stepson Charles Smithers and my stepdaughter Susan Smithers.

As Witness my hand the day and year first above written.

Signed by the said testator in the presence of us, present at the same time, who at his request and in his presence have subscribed our names as witnesses.

Arthur B. Bloggins

Adam Smith

of 2 The Cottages,
Blacktown
(Bricklayer)

Milton Freeman

of 3 Smallacre,
Blacktown
(Motor Mechanic)

This Will assumes that all the children and grandchildren involved are over 18. Otherwise, see sample Will 10.

18) *A person wishing to leave land, specific items and also pecuniary legacies to certain persons.*

This is the last Will and Testament of me Arthur Bruce Bloggins of 1, Whiteacre, Blacktown in the County of Greenshire, made this . . . day of . . . , one thousand nine hundred and . . .

I hereby revoke all former Wills made by me and declare this to be my last Will.

I appoint my brother Richard Bloggins and my sister Amanda Bloggins to be the executors of this my Will.

I devise my freehold land and property, excluding the contents thereof, at 1, Whiteacre, Blacktown, in the County of Greenshire to my brother Richard Bloggins absolutely, free of all encumbrances.

I give the following bequests:

1. To my sister Amanda Bloggins I bequeath my collection of stamps.
2. To my brother Richard Bloggins I bequeath my antique grandfather clock which, at the time of making this my Will, stands in the hallway of 1, Whiteacre, Blacktown, aforesaid.

I give the following pecuniary legacies:

1. To my housekeeper Mrs. Patience Char I bequeath the sum of one thousand pounds (£1,000) free of tax.
2. To my sister Amanda Bloggins I bequeath the sum of five thousand pounds (£5,000) free of tax.

After payment of all my testamentary and funeral expenses and liability for Inheritance or other tax I devise and bequeath all my real and personal estate whatsoever and wheresoever to the charity Save Our Souls Society, or such other charity as my executors may in their absolute discretion decide, and I declare that the receipt of the person professing to be the treasurer or other duly authorised officer of the said Society shall be deemed a full and sufficient discharge to my executors who shall not be bound to see the application thereof.

As Witness my hand the day and year first above written.

Signed by the said testator in the
presence of us, present at the
same time, who at his request
and in his presence have
subscribed our names as
witnesses.

Arthur B. Bloggins

Adam Smith

of 2 The Cottages,
Blacktown
(Bricklayer)

Milton Freeman

of 3 Smallacre,
Blacktown
(Motor Mechanic)

19) A person wishing to dispose of his business to his son:

This is the last Will and Testament of me Arthur Bruce Bloggins of 1, Whiteacre, Blacktown in the County of Greenshire, made this . . . day of . . . , one thousand nine hundred and . . .

I hereby revoke all former Wills made by me and declare this to be my last Will.

I appoint my wife Ann Belinda Bloggins and my son Charles Alan Bloggins to be the executors of this my Will.

I devise and bequeath my freehold business premises, the business machinery and all items, vehicles, office furniture, and equipment appurtenant thereto together with the goodwill of my business as a baker situate at The Granary, Barley Lane, Blacktown, to my son Charles Alan Bloggins absolutely, provided that he discharges any liability to Inheritance Tax thereon.

After payment of my testamentary and funeral expenses devise and bequeath the residue of all my real and personal estate whatsoever and wheresoever to my wife Ann Belinda Bloggins absolutely if she shall survive me by 30 days or, in the event of her not surviving me by 30 days to my son Charles Alan Bloggins absolutely.

As Witness my hand the day and year first above written.

Signed by the said testator in the
presence of us, present at the
same time, who at his request
and in his presence have
subscribed our names as
witnesses.

Arthur B. Bloggins

Adam Smith

of 2 The Cottages,
Blacktown
(Bricklayer)

Milton Freeman

of 3 Smallacre,
Blacktown
(Motor Mechanic)

20) *A person wishing to leave everything to his wife and his body for spare-part surgery or for medical research or education.*

This is the last Will and Testament of me Arthur Bruce Bloggins of 1, Whiteacre, Blacktown in the County of Greenshire, made this . . . day of . . ., one thousand nine hundred and . . .

I hereby revoke all former Wills made by me and declare this to be my last Will.

I appoint my wife Ann Belinda Bloggins to be my sole executrix of this my Will, except that, if she shall not survive me by thirty days then I appoint Messrs. Smith, Jones and Browne of Peradventure Passage, Blacktown, to be my executors, who shall be entitled to charge and be paid out of the residue of my estate, all professional or other charges for all business or acts done by them in connection with this my Will.

I devise and bequeath all my real and personal estate whatsoever and wheresoever to my wife Ann Belinda Bloggins absolutely if she shall survive me by 30 days.

If she shall not survive me by 30 days my estate is to go to the Save Our Souls Society or such other charity or charities and in such proportions as my executors in their absolute discretion shall decide. I declare that the receipt of the person professing to be the treasurer or other duly authorised officer of the said Society shall be deemed a full and sufficient discharge to my executors who shall not be bound to see to the application thereof.

I desire and authorise after my death the use of any part or parts of my body for therapeutic purposes (including corneal grafting and transplantation) or for purposes of medical research or education. I desire that, after the removal of any part or parts for the said purposes, my body shall be cremated and I authorise either my executrix or executors or any hospital or other institution which has charge of my body to make arrangements for the said cremation. I further authorise my executrix or executors to spend out of my estate as much money as in her or their absolute discretion she or they think fit in order to carry out my wishes as expressed above.

As Witness my hand the day and year first above written.

Signed by the said testator in the
presence of us, present at the
same time, who at his request
and in his presence have
subscribed our names as
witnesses.

Arthur B. Bloggins

Adam Smith

of 2 The Cottages,
Blacktown
(Bricklayer)

Milton Freeman

of 3 Smallacre,
Blacktown
(Motor Mechanic)

*NOTE: If you wish to leave your body for therapeutic purposes
eg. spare-part surgery and not for medical research or
education then you should delete ". . . or for purposes of
medical or education" and you should add:*

**"For the avoidance of doubt I desire that my body shall not
be used for the purposes of medical research or education."**

The rest can remain the same.

*Do remember that it is important that you tell someone,
usually your next of kin, of your wishes so that they can
be implemented immediately on your death. Otherwise,
by the time your Will is read it will probably be too late
for your body to be put to any useful purpose.*

Continued overleaf

Continued from previous page

If you are concerned that parts of your body might be removed when, in fact, you are not dead then you should add the following clause:

"I direct my executors to take all steps and engage and pay all doctors or other persons as they in their absolute discretion think are necessary in order to ensure that I am in fact dead and not merely appearing to be dead."

In order for this to have effect you must, of course, tell your executors that this is your wish, preferably by showing them a copy of the Will before your death so that, on your death, they can put your wishes into effect. You will appreciate that this is easier for executors who are relations who will probably learn about your death before your solicitors do.

21) *A person wishing to have his property disposed of according to the law of intestacy (as set out in Chapter 8, page 108) but wanting to revoke all previous Wills.*

This is the last Will and Testament of me Arthur Bruce Bloggins of 1, Whiteacre, Blacktown in the County of Greenshire, made this . . . day of . . ., one thousand nine hundred and . . .

I hereby revoke all former Wills made by me and declare this to be my last Will.

I appoint my wife Ann Belinda Bloggins to be the sole executrix of this my Will.

I desire that all my real and personal estate whatsoever and wheresoever shall be disposed of according to the rules of intestacy and I make no dispositions thereof.

As Witness my hand the day and year first above written.

Signed by the said testator
in the presence of us,
present at the same time,
who at his request and in
his presence have
subscribed our names as
witnesses.

Arthur B. Bloggins

Adam Smith

of 2 The Cottages,
Blacktown
(Bricklayer)

Milton Freeman

of 3 Smallacre,
Blacktown
(Motor Mechanic)

8

WHO BENEFITS IF I MAKE NO WILL?

Where a person dies without leaving a Will their property is disposed of according to the law of intestacy (from the Latin meaning "no Will").

In Chapter 10 (page 113) we shall see how certain persons, such as surviving spouse, children and other dependants, can claim money from the estate whether there is a Will or not. Everything that is stated in this chapter on intestacy is still subject to any claims that may be made by these persons.

It may be, of course, that a person decides that he wants to die without specifically disposing of his property so that, in fact, his property is disposed of according to the law of intestacy. In this case it is sensible to make a Will declaring one's desire to die intestate since this will have the effect of revoking any previous Will, and a sample Will of this kind is shown on page 107.

Where a person dies without making a Will, or without making a fresh Will having revoked an earlier one, then the person's property is disposed of according to what family he leaves. All the property is held by the personal representative so that it can be sold and the proceeds distributed according to the rules that are set out below. The personal representative has the power to postpone the sale. Personal items as defined on page 61 must not be sold unless it is necessary to do so in order to pay for the administration of the estate.

Once the funeral expenses and administration costs have been paid the property is distributed as follows:—

1. If there is a surviving spouse (husband or wife) and there are no children or other descendants, no parents living, no brothers or sisters, or their children living then the surviving spouse receives all the property absolutely.
2. If there is a surviving spouse (husband or wife) and there are children (whether or not there are any parents, brothers or sisters or their children) then the surviving spouse receives:

a) all personal items together with,

b) £75,000 (if that much is available) plus interest at 6% p.a. from death. In addition to this the surviving spouse receives,

c) a life interest in half the residue of the estate. The residue of the estate is what is left once the personal items and the £75,000 and other expenses have been taken out. A life interest means that he or she does not get the absolute ownership of one half of the residue of the estate, but has a right to it and can use it for the rest of his or her life. Consequently, a life interest means that a surviving spouse is entitled to the income from the money but not allowed to spend the money itself. The other half of the residue is split up amongst the children and is given to them absolutely. When the surviving spouse dies these children then become entitled absolutely in equal shares to the half of the residue of which he or she has had the use during his or her life.

3. If there is a surviving spouse (husband or wife) and there are no children but there are parents, brothers or sisters or children of brothers or sisters then the surviving spouse receives:

a) all personal items together with,

b) £125,000 (if available) plus interest at 6% p.a. from death. In addition to this the surviving spouse receives:

c) half the residue of the estate absolutely. If there is a parent or parents then the parent(s) receives the other half of the residue absolutely in equal shares. If there is no parent then this half goes to the brothers and sisters in equal shares.

4. If there is no surviving spouse then the estate is held for the children so that all shall have equal shares when they reach the age of eighteen or marry, whichever is the sooner. But if certain children have been given gifts during the lifetime of the person who has died, then they may find their share cut down by the amount that they have received prior to the person's death.

In this context when dealing with intestacy the word children means and includes illegitimate children and adopted children, so long as there has been a formal adoption order. Children who have been loosely "adopted" without a formal adoption order will not be included. The word children does not include step-children, and they will receive nothing if a person dies intestate.

5. If there is no surviving spouse and no children but one or two parents then the parent(s) receives the estate absolutely in equal shares.

6. If there is no surviving spouse, no children and no parents then the residue of the estate is disposed of in the following order:

   a) brothers and sisters absolutely, but if none then:
   b) half-brothers and half-sisters, but if none then:
   c) grandparent or grandparents, but if none then:
   d) uncles and aunts of the whole blood (that is brothers and sisters of a parent of the person who has died), but if none then:
   e) uncles and aunts of the half blood (that is half-brothers and half-sisters of a parent of the person who has died).

   In all these items a) to e) where there is more than one of the persons specified then the residue is shared equally by however many there may be.

Children, brothers, sisters, uncles and aunts who die before the date of death of the person dying intestate are represented by their descendants, so that their share goes to their children.

You will notice that there is no provision for a mistress or co-habitee or common law wife as she is sometimes known, that is, a woman who is living with someone but not married to them. She is not entitled to anything under the law according to intestacy, but she may be able to claim under the Inheritance (Provision for Family and Dependants) Act 1975, see Chapter 10 (page 113).

Where there has been a divorce the divorced surviving spouse is not entitled to anything under these rules and loses all rights. Divorce dates from the grant of decree absolute.

Where two people who are married have been granted an order of judicial separation in the Divorce County Court then, on one of them dying without leaving a Will, the other will *not* be entitled as the surviving spouse according to the law of intestacy. Yet where two people who are married have been granted an order in the Magistrates' Court that they are no longer bound to live with one another then, on one of them dying without leaving a Will, the other one *will* be entitled as the surviving spouse according to the law of intestacy, just like any other surviving spouse.

A surviving spouse has the right to have included as part of his/her entitlement under the above rules any house or flat which is part of the residual estate in which he/she was living at the time of the death. This is so as to ensure that a surviving spouse can stay on in the matrimonial home.

Where children are entitled to receive something under the rules stated above, but have died themselves, then their children are entitled to it, whether they are legitimate or illegitimate.

Conclusion

As you can see, if you do not make a Will, you have no control over your property after your death and it can be dealt with in a way totally different from what you might have wished.

9

GIFTS IN CONTEMPLATION OF MARRIAGE

The general rule is that marriage revokes a Will made before the marriage so that it no longer has any effect (but it is different in Scotland, see Chapter 13, page 142). If, however, the Will makes it clear that a marriage is intended to a particular person and that it is intended that the marriage should not have the effect of revoking it then the Will remains valid after the marriage and will take effect on the death of the person making it. It is most important to specify in the Will the name of the person whom it is intended to marry. Merely stating that the Will is made "in contemplation of marriage" or other generalisation is insufficient. It is also important to specify in the Will that you intend the Will to remain valid after the marriage. This is true of all the provisions in the Will unless it is made clear in the Will that it is intended that any particular provision should be revoked by marriage. You should read Chapter 5, page 33.

10

HOW CAN THE COURT INTERVENE (1)?

What if You Made a Mistake?

The Court now has wide powers to make a Will accord with the intentions of the person who made it if it fails to do so as a result of a clerical error or a failure to understand his instructions. This is called rectifying the Will and consists of altering the wording so that it has the effect of according with the testator's intentions. It involves an application to the Court but, except with the Court's permission, this must be made within six months of the date on which probate is first taken out. So if your Will is ambiguous or misleading it is not necessarily a disaster which would make you turn in your grave although, of course, it is better not to have to rely on a Court to put matters right! Your personal representatives or executors can put their minds at rest, as well, because they are not held liable for having distributed any part of the estate after the end of six months from the date on which probate is first taken out if it turns out that such a distribution was not the intention of the testator. The beneficiaries, or people who receive such a distribution, however, should beware! The Court can recover any property distributed if it decides to rectify the Will!

If any part of a Will is meaningless or the language is ambiguous in itself or in the light of surrounding circumstances then the Court will look at the surrounding evidence, including evidence of the testator's intention, in order to interpret the Will. This is where any letters you leave or conversations you may have had expressing your intentions could be important after your death.

One further matter should be mentioned in respect of a Will that is not quite clear. Where the Will devises or bequeaths property to the testator's husband or wife in absolute terms but also tries to leave an interest in the same property to the testator's children then the husband or wife takes the property absolutely despite the attempted gift to the children.

The Right to Dispose of Your Property

In general, the law allows an unfettered right to dispose of one's property as a person chooses, subject to the question of tax and to the powers of the court to intervene. It is this last restriction that we shall now examine in greater detail.

Many people are very surprised when they learn what broad powers the courts have for intervening. These powers have been increasing over the years. As we shall see the courts can disrupt a person's intentions to dispose of his property in two ways: by providing for certain people who may or may not be catered for in the Will (this Chapter) and by declaring that leaving property with certain conditions attached is contrary to public policy and therefore should not be allowed (see Chapter 11, page 120).

Up until 1938 a person could dispose of his property as he liked without having regard to any moral obligation that he might have after his death to people who depended upon him or who had given years of unpaid service. Thus, the dedicated daughter who devoted her life to looking after her aged mother rather than sending her to an institution could find herself left with nothing when her mother died if, in the Will, her mother wanted to exclude her.

Since 1938 the situation has been different, and it is important to know what provision that courts can order, since, for many people, the object of making a Will is just as much to *exclude* people from getting anything as it is to ensure that people are properly provided for!

The law has now been consolidated in the Inheritance (Provision for Family and Dependants) Act, 1975. Certain persons can now apply to the court to be given money out of the deceased's estate. This can be done whether there was a Will or not. Obviously, where there is a Will then the Court's powers will interfere with it, but it will give comfort to relations of a person who dies without making a Will, since they can now be provided for.

The court's powers are very wide. The husband or wife of the deceased person can be given any amount of money that the court thinks is reasonable, even if they do not need it to maintain themselves in paying for everyday living expenses. The 1975 Act implements the recommendations of the Law Commission which felt that a surviving spouse (husband or wife of the deceased person) should be given money out of the estate on the same principles as a spouse is given money when there is a divorce. Now this can mean that if Mr. Bloggins dies, either without making a Will or having made a Will which leaves nothing to his surviving wife, then she can apply to the court for money out of Mr. Bloggins' estate. Even if she does

not need the money to live on, Mrs Bloggins can still be
awarded a large part of Mr. Bloggins' estate. In fact, although
it varies and there is no hard and fast rule, Mrs. Bloggins could
get as much as half Mr. Bloggins' estate and this, remember,
where Mr. Bloggins might have deliberately excluded her from
his Will because he did not want her to receive anything!

The situation is different, however, for other relations.
Although they can apply to the Court where there is either a
Will or no Will the money they can get out of the estate will be
only so much as the Court considers necessary for their
maintenance, that is payment for everyday living expenses.

One other point is that where the deceased's estate is
insolvent, which means that the claims of debts on it are greater
than the assets, then no claim can be made by anyone.

The following people can claim:—

1. The wife or husband of the deceased;
2. A former wife or former husband of the deceased who
   has not remarried;
3. A child of the deceased;
4. Any person who is not included as a child of the deceased,
   but who was treated by the deceased as a child of the
   family in relation to any marriage during his lifetime;
5. Any other person who was being maintained, even if only
   partly maintained, by the deceased just before his death.

Category 1 includes a person who enters into a marriage in
good faith but it is, in fact, void. For example, Mr. Bloggins
may be married already, but he enters into a bigamous (and
therefore void) marriage with Mrs. Smith. Mrs. Smith acts in
good faith and thinks that Mr. Bloggins is free to marry. If Mr.
Bloggins dies then Mrs. Smith can still claim under Category 1
as the surviving spouse, so long as the marriage is not annulled
and/or Mrs. Smith does not marry again in Mr. Bloggins'
lifetime. It is interesting to note that after Mr. Bloggins' death
she can still claim under Category 1 even if she remarries, so
long as she remarries after and not before, Mr. Bloggins' death,
although her remarriage will probably affect the amount she
may be awarded. If the Court makes an order for her
maintenance by way of periodical payments, however, they
terminate on her death or if she remarries.

Categories 2 and 3 are self-explanatory, but we must spend a
little more space on Categories 4 and 5. Category 4 includes
any child who was treated as a child of the family by the
deceased, whether or not that child was *actually* a child of the

deceased. The following example will illustrate: Mrs. Smith is a divorced woman who has one daughter, Abigail, by Mr. Smith her former husband. One day Mrs. Smith meets Mr. Bloggins and they are married and have one child, Bertie. All four of them live together and Mr. Bloggins provides a home, food and schooling for Abigail, although she is not his child, and treats her in the same way as he does his own child, Bertie. In fact, he is said to treat Abigail as "a child of the family". After a while, however, Mrs. Smith goes off with another man, takes Abigail and Bertie with her and is divorced from Mr. Bloggins. Mr. Bloggins is heartbroken, but finds consolation in the company of Mrs. Brown, a divorcee who has her own child Belinda by a former marriage. Mr. Bloggins marries Mrs. Brown and together with Belinda they live as a family and Mr. Bloggins treats Belinda as he would his own child. Mr. Bloggins dies.

Who can apply to the Court for money out of Mr. Bloggins' estate?

Clearly, Mrs. Brown can claim (under Category 1) because she is the surviving spouse.

Mrs. Smith can claim also because, although she went off with another man, she has not remarried. Consequently, she comes under Category 2.

Bertie is Mr. Bloggins' own child and so can claim under Category 3.

Under Category 4 both Abigail and Belinda can claim, although they are not Mr. Bloggins' own children. Both however, were treated by Mr. Bloggins as children of the family and are included because they were children of a marriage of Mr. Bloggins although they were by different marriages.

Category 4 also includes an illegitimate child and a child conceived and being carried by its mother, but not yet born, at the date of the deceased's death.

We must now deal with Category 5 which is very broad and includes all persons who were partly dependent upon the deceased just before his death. You will have noticed that Categories 1 and 2 deal only with spouses: to be included in these categories there must have been a marriage, so a person merely cohabiting with the deceased before his death is not included in Categories 1 and 2. Even though they may have been living together as man and wife, if they were not actually married then the surviving person cannot be regarded as the wife or husband or a former wife or husband. A person living with the deceased can claim, however, under Category 5 so long as he or she was being partly or wholly maintained by the deceased just before his death.

As we have noted already, the practical difference between Category 1 (surviving husband or wife) and the other categories including Category 5, is that under Category 1 a surviving husband or wife can claim much more than just the amount needed to maintain him or her whereas under the other categories all that can be claimed is maintenance, or sufficient to pay everyday living expenses which are considered reasonable by the Court.

If a husband or wife is divorced or judicially separated from the deceased then, of course, he or she is entitled to claim only maintenance and not the higher amount which is allowed to a surviving spouse. Nevertheless, if the husband or wife was divorced or judicially separated within twelve months of the deceased's death then a special concession is made: in these circumstances he or she can claim the higher amount.

So, in order to claim under Category 5 a person need show only that he or she was being maintained by the deceased, either wholly or partly, just before his death. This means that the deceased must have been making a substantial contribution towards the reasonable needs of that person. It does not have to be in money: it can be in providing board and accommodation. Moreover, *anyone* who was being partly maintained can apply: it is not necessary to be a relation of the deceased. The following are examples of what "maintained" can mean: an elderly housekeeper may receive food, shelter, warmth and clothing in return for purely nominal services; a nephew may be attending school at the expense of the deceased; a widowed sister may be receiving board and lodging in the home of the deceased but making some contribution in cash to the expenses of the home. All those people could be said to be partly or wholly maintained by the deceased and so would be able to claim.

In a case in 1977 it was decided that a sister was entitled to claim in the following circumstances: Miss N. was employed up to 1969 when she left to go to live with her sister Miss W. Miss W., who had suffered from arthritis, had put considerable pressure on her sister's employer to encourage her to leave and live with her. When Miss N. went to live with her in 1969 she received free board and lodging and she shared household duties and cooking with Miss W. who at that time was reasonably active. The heavy housework was done by a home help. Miss W. had paid all the outgoings such as the household expenses and rates and from 1973 until Miss W.'s death in May, 1976, Miss N. had done an equal share of light housework and cooking. She had been available to Miss W. as a companion in the sense that Miss W. would not be lonely. The court felt that the light housework and cooking that Miss N. did could not be regarded as payment for the board and lodging she received from Miss W. Consequently, Miss N. was entitled to claim on Miss W.'s estate.

Let us assume, in another example, that Mr. and Mrs. Bloggins and their son live together with Mrs. Bloggins' mother. Mr. Bloggins cannot stand his mother-in-law who he feels interferes too much with his marriage and always takes his wife's side. On the insistence of his wife, however, Mr. Bloggins agreed that his mother-in-law should live with them and not pay any rent. When making his Will Mr. Bloggins specifically excludes his mother-in-law, since she is the last person he would want to benefit from his death. In fact, he leaves all his money to his wife and son equally. Mr. Bloggins dies, but, under Category 5 his mother-in-law can make a claim against his estate and is entitled to receive a reasonable amount of money for her maintenance from the estate. Under the court's powers this can be paid as a lump sum payment, or as periodical payments (that is, weekly or monthly, etc. payments) or by giving his mother-in-law part of Mr. Bloggins' property.

This means, of course, that there will be less money in the estate to be divided between his wife and son in accordance with his wishes. The court has power to decide how the payment to his mother-in-law will be made and also, whether that money will be taken wholly out of his wife's share, or wholly out of his son's share, or whether part of it should come from his wife's share and part of it from his son's share.

Now you may feel that if Mr. Bloggins realised that his mother-in-law could claim he should have stated in his Will, that if she did claim against the estate, how that claim could be met. Thus, if Mr. Bloggins wanted to ensure that his wife had half his estate in any event then perhaps he could state in his Will that any claim by his mother-in-law should be satisfied out of his son's share. I am afraid that this will not do, because even if Mr. Bloggins expresses this in his Will it is still open to the court to apportion his mother-in-law's share as it thinks fit.

As you can imagine, there will be many people who will try to get round the 1975 Act and its provision for relations and dependants, but I have to tell you that Parliament has thought of some of the dodges and deals with them in the Act. If it can be shown to the court that, less than six years before his death, the deceased gave away some of his property or money with the intention of defeating an application by anyone for the financial provision under the 1975 Act, then the court can order that property or money to be given back.

The person who has received the gift can be made to pay all or some of it back even though he has disposed of it himself and no longer has it. In the case of money, which includes an insurance premium, he cannot be made to pay back more than the amount of money he has received less anything he has had to pay in Inheritance Tax. In the case of property (either land or other property) he cannot be made to pay back more than the value of the property at the time of the deceased's death less anything he has had to pay in Inheritance Tax. For tax considerations generally, see Chapter 12.

Obviously, this can work very harshly against an innocent party as the following example may show. In order to defeat any claim that his mother-in-law may have, Mr. Bloggins decides to dispose of some of his assets during his lifetime. In May 1985 he gives his house over to his wife. In June 1985 he gives his car over to his son. His son, however, has got a car already, so his son gives away the car to a friend. In July 1985 Mr. Bloggins gives £3,000 to his own mother who is a senior citizen on limited means and who spends the money on a new carpet and having her small flat redecorated. A year later Mr. Bloggins dies. As was to be expected, his mother-in-law, who was living with the family rent free but who has received nothing else from Mr. Bloggins, makes an application to the court for maintenance as she was a dependant. Now I stress that it is entirely up to the court what order it makes, but it *could* order the following: Mrs. Bloggins to pay back the value of the house at the date of Mr. Bloggins' death; his son to pay back the value of the car at the date of Mr. Bloggins' death, less any Inheritance Tax he has paid, even though he no longer has the car; and Mr. Bloggins' aged mother could be ordered to pay back £3,000 less any Inheritance Tax she has paid, even though she has spent the money. The net result could be the loss of a roof over Mrs. Bloggins' head and financial ruin for Mr. Bloggins' son and mother.

It is important to remember that these provisions apply only to *gifts*; they do not apply where the item has been paid for, according to its value. So if Mrs. Bloggins had paid her husband for the house and his son had paid him for the car then they would not be liable to pay back anything, unless it was said that they had paid less than the value of the items. The test is whether "valuable consideration" has been given by the person who has received the money or property. If valuable consideration has been given then it is not a gift and the person receiving the money or property will not be liable to pay back. Valuable consideration does not mean just giving money for the item. It can be in other forms. Thus, if Mr. Bloggins owed his mother £4,000 and he gave her the £3,000 on the basis that she would forget about the £4,000 then her agreeing not to claim the full £4,000 debt would be valuable consideration, and in the circumstances of the example above she would not be liable to pay back the £3,000.

It is also worth remembering that the courts must be satisfied that the deceased made the gift with the intention of defeating a claim under the 1975 Act. It must be shown that it was the deceased's intention, though not necessarily his sole intention, either to prevent or to reduce a payment being made to a spouse or dependant on a claim under the 1975 Act. Suppose the deceased made a contract with someone by which he agreed to leave in his Will a sum of money or other property. If no valuable consideration was given by that person or anyone else at the time of the contract, then, unless it is shown to the contrary, the court presumes that the contract was made with the intention of defeating a claim under the 1975 Act. It then means that the person with whom the contract was made will have to prove that the deceased did not, in fact, have that intention.

So, if you decide you want to evade the provisions of the 1975 Act by giving away some or all of your assets before you die, beware! You have been warned! You may, in fact, create great difficulties for those people to whom you give money or other property.

A person who wants to make a claim as a spouse or dependant under the 1975 Act has to do so within six months of a Grant of Probate or Letters of Administration.

Everything that has been stated above applies only to Wills made in England and Wales; it does not apply to Scotland nor to Northern Ireland.

11

HOW CAN THE COURT INTERVENE (II)?

This chapter deals with conditions that are attached to gifts. This is a way in which the person making the Will can try to get people to do things after his death by ensuring that there will be no gift unless the condition is fulfilled. It can be a powerful weapon since, if it is reasonable, most people will want to carry out the conditions in order to receive the gift. A gift can also be conditional on something happening. As you may imagine, the courts have scrutinized very carefully such conditions over the years.

The problem arises when conditions attached to the gifts, or dispositions, of the testator (the person making the Will) are regarded as *contrary to public policy* and therefore are not allowed. If a condition is disallowed in this way, then it is void, that is, of no effect. The consequences of this on the gift in the Will are described at the end of this chapter.

It is impossible to give a comprehensive list of what conditions would be disallowed by the court since these matters are decided by the court as and when they come before it. The examples that are given below are taken from actual cases so that we can say with near certainty that, in future, similar conditions would be disallowed. On other matters we can only apply general principles to see if it is likely that they will be disallowed.

The overall principle governing the court's approach is whether the condition attached to the gift is contrary to public policy. In more strictly moral times in this country it was felt that gifts to illegitimate children were against public policy because they tended to encourage immorality; but since the 1930's that rigid view has been relaxed. Certainly, a gift that encourages the breakdown of marriage would be regarded as against public policy and would not be valid: Mr. Bloggins in his Will would not be able to leave money to his married daughter on condition of her divorcing her husband because that would encourage the breaking up of her marriage. Similarly, although Mr. Bloggins could leave money to his *own* illegitimate children, he would not be allowed to leave money to someone else's illegitimate child to be conceived after his death, because that would encourage sexual intercourse outside marriage. For example, a gift by Mr. Bloggins would be disallowed if it was to any illegitimate children conceived by his wife after his death. In the words of a Victorian judge, this sort of gift "would, I think, manifestly encourage the immoral connection and discourage marriage, which the law favours."

Public Policy and Marriage and the Family
Apart from the situations described above the following are examples where the court has intervened over the question of marriage and the family and public policy.

In a 1966 case a testator (the person making the Will) in his Will directed that the income from his estate should be held on trust for his daughter, who was married with two children and was living with her husband. The testator further directed, amongst other conditions, that his daughter should not receive more than £50 per year and that the balance left over, between the £50 and the income from his estate, should be accumulated. He further stated that if his daughter's husband should die, or if they were divorced or were to live separately then his daughter should receive the whole of the income, not just limited to £50, together with any money that had accumulated. When the case came to court the judge decided that it was a situation "which would tend to encourage the daughter to separate from her husband or possibly to divorce him which it seems to me this court cannot allow". The income from the whole estate was far more than just £50 so there was a financial incentive for the daughter to break up the marriage, which is against public policy.

Sometimes, Wills of this kind are made by the testator out of personal dislike for someone and are done, with a view to breaking up a marriage deliberately, whereas others may have that effect but may not necessarily be intended to have that effect. The intention of the testator has little to do with whether a court decides a provision in a Will is against public policy or not. So if you make a Will which has the effect of encouraging someone's marriage to break up by giving a financial incentive, then the court may decide that it is void and will have no force, even though you may not have intended it to encourage a marriage to break up.

Yet, where a marriage has broken up already, it seems that a provision in a Will which might provide a financial incentive for the wife not to go back to her husband will not be contrary to public policy. In an earlier case, in 1920, the testator was a married man living with a married woman, someone else's wife. In his Will he gave her £750 a year (a large sum of money in those days) provided she was still living with him at his death and the £750 per year would continue provided she did not return to live with her own husband or remarry and that she led a clean moral and responsible life. In this case the court decided that the provision was not against public policy since its object was not to induce the lady to continue to live apart from her husband but was to maintain her until she returned to her husband or remarried.

A provision can still be declared void for being contrary to public policy even when it has only the indirect effect of breaking up a marriage. Thus, a condition was void which took away a gift to a married woman unless she ceased to reside in Skipton which was where her husband both worked and lived. The court felt that such a condition induced her not to carry out her duties as a wife.

Similarly, provisions which give a financial incentive not to get married at all are also regarded as contrary to public policy, but only where they inhibit marriage altogether. Mere restrictions on getting married, however, are not against public policy. There is no objection to the following conditions against a marriage:

Mr. Bloggins leaves property to A on condition that he does not marry his housekeeper or anyone who has been his housekeeper: that is valid.

Mr. Bloggins leaves property to A on condition that he does not marry without the consent of B: that is valid.

Mr. Bloggins leaves property to A on condition that he does not remarry if his present marriage should come to an end: that is valid.

Mr. Bloggins leaves property to A on condition that he does not marry anyone who is not a Jew: that is valid.

Mr. Bloggins leaves property to A on condition that he does not marry anyone not born in Scotland nor of Scottish parents: that is valid.

These are just examples of cases that have been decided. There is nothing magic in the conditions relating to Jews or

Scots and any similar provisions would be valid.

Furthermore, when a Will makes provision for someone *until* they marry that is not regarded as contrary to public policy because it is designed to look after someone until they marry and not to prevent marriage altogether.

If Mr. Bloggins leaves £500 a year to his daughter until she marries that will be regarded as valid by the court.

A condition on a gift restricting marriage until after a certain age, even as high as 28, is regarded as valid because it does not prevent marriage altogether. If Mr. Bloggins leaves £1,000 to his son on condition that he does not marry until he is aged 25, that will be regarded as valid.

A husband or wife can impose a condition in his or her Will that the surviving spouse should receive something under the Will so long as he or she does not remarry, and such a condition will be valid. But where the gift is of a specific item then the condition should also state what will happen to the item if the surviving spouse does remarry.

There is a reason why the court allows a husband or wife in his/her Will to impose a condition that a gift under the Will should either cease altogether or be diminished if the surviving husband or wife should remarry. The reason is that for over a hundred years the court has realised that a husband or wife has a special interest in whether the surviving spouse should remarry or not. Remember, a condition preventing marriage of anyone else other than the surviving spouse would be void.

We have seen that a condition on a gift is invalid if it induces a separation of husband and wife, because that is against public policy. But there is nothing to stop Mr. Bloggins leaving property to his married daughter if her husband divorces her, because that would provide for her in the event of divorce, it would not induce her to break up the marriage since the condition specifies that it would be her husband who divorces her, not she who divorces her husband. Conditions on gifts that persons separate are only invalid where those persons are married. There is nothing wrong with a gift conditional on cohabitees or even friends parting from one another, subject to the following section.

Thus, a gift by Mr. Bloggins on condition that his daughter separates from her husband is not valid. But a gift on condition that his daughter separates from her boyfriend or her girlfriend, is perfectly valid.

Let us now look at an example which covers some of these ideas and see if we can discern which conditions are valid and which are not.

In his Will Mr. Bloggins makes the following gifts:

£5,000 to his wife on condition that she never remarries.

£1,000 to his married daughter Jane on condition that she leaves her husband whom Mr. Bloggins does not like.

£500 a year to George if he never marries.

£500 a year to Susan if she does not marry before she has finished her training as a teacher and only marries another teacher.

£100 to George's three illegitimate children plus £100 to any further illegitimate child conceived after Mr. Bloggins' death.

£200 a year to his sister Alfreda for as long as she remains separated from her husband from whom she has been separated for some time.

£50 to his niece Tina on condition that she separates from her boyfriend who Mr. Bloggins thinks is a bad lot.

Do you think that you have the correct answers? The gift to his wife is valid. The gift to Jane is invalid since it induces the breaking up of her marriage. The gift to George is invalid since he can never marry if he is to receive his £500 a year. The gift to Susan, however, is valid because that merely restricts her marriage. The gifts to George's illegitimate children are valid, but not to any further illegitimate children since they have not yet been conceived and it encourages George to have sexual intercourse outside marriage. The gift to Alfreda will take effect since it is merely providing for her until she returns to her husband, if she ever does. Finally, the gift to Tina will be upheld because it does not induce the separation of people who are married.

Public Policy and Parents and Children
Conditions which provide for children being separated from their parents are void since it is against public policy that they should be split up. Anything that induces this will be void; even a condition which requires children to live in a certain part of the country will be invalid if its effect is to part them from their parents. This only applies to children who are still largely dependent upon their parents: it does not apply to adult children and the court has decided that a condition was valid

which said that an adult child should not live with her mother.

In a case earlier this century a testator in his Will gave a gift to his two grand-children but inserted the condition that if either one or both of the grand-children should "live with or be or continue under the custody, guardianship or control of their father . . . or be in any way directly under his control" then the gift should not take effect. The court decided that this was contrary to public policy because it was inserted with the object of deterring the father from performing his parental duties. Even if this condition had not been contrary to public policy it would still not have taken effect, because it was too uncertain. Who can say what "under his control" means? Does it mean that the grandchildren should not see their father, because it could be said that by seeing them he was influencing and controlling them? Or does it mean that the father must not even write a letter to them because it might be said that writing to them was influencing them and putting them under their father's control? You can see that where a condition defies interpretation like this one, then that condition will be invalid whether it is contrary to public policy or not.

Public Policy and Religion

Conditions imposed on gifts and concerning religion, such as a gift to someone on condition that they become a member of or cease to be a member of a certain religion, are not against public policy. You must be careful, though, to ensure that the condition is very clear since many conditions concerning religion have been declared void in the past because they have been uncertain. We must look at this in a little more detail. The situation can be complex and the dividing line is very thin between what condition the court considers is ascertainable and certain, and therefore valid, and what condition is uncertain, and therefore void.

Some examples of cases demonstrate the difficulties:

> Mr. K. in his Will left part of his estate on trust to his daughter provided that she should receive nothing if, either during his lifetime or after his death, she married a "person who does not practise the Jewish religion". One year after Mr. K.'s death his daughter married Mr. O'D. who was not a Jew by birth.

For some time before the marriage Mr. O'D. had participated in and observed the ritual of the Jewish religion which he saw in the home of Mr. K.'s daughter, and he had accompanied them to the synagogue on a number of occasions. Shortly after the marriage he was formally received into the Jewish religion and, some eight months after the marriage, he and Mr. K.'s daughter went through another ceremony of marriage, this time according to Jewish rites.

One of the questions that came before the court was whether the condition on the gift that the daughter should receive nothing if she married a person who did not practise the Jewish religion was void for uncertainty. The judge said ". . . the gift is void. I do not know, except in the broadest and most indefinite sense, what is meant by 'practising' the Jewish religion, or, indeed, any religion, and the expression seems to me to lack altogether that precision which is essential . . .".

So the condition was void, not because a condition about marrying a Jew is against public policy, but because "practising the Jewish religion" is far too vague and uncertain. It is impossible for any court to be able to say whether a person is "practising" a certain religion. Perhaps the majority of people in this country are still Christian, or have sympathy with Christian ideals, but who can say with any certainty which of them "practise" Christianity? "Practise" defies definition.

Similarly, where Mr. I. gave £250 to each of his grandsons and £500 to each of his grand-daughters on condition that they married "according to the rites of the Jewish faith a person of Jewish race and religion" such a condition was void for uncertainty because it would be impossible for a court to decide who was a person "of Jewish race". It is open to many interpretations. Does "Jewish race" mean that both one's parents have to be Jewish, or just one parent, or that one has to be born in Israel? Once again, you can see that it is incapable of precise definition.

A condition in a Will which requires a person before he can take his gift under the Will to be confirmed as a member of the Church of England is valid because confirmation is a definite act and can easily be ascertained.

A gift on condition that children are brought up in the Protestant faith is invalid for two reasons. The first is that the "Protestant faith" is too vague and the condition, therefore, is void for uncertainty. Secondly, because it is the duty of a parent to bring children up in the particular religion which he or she thinks best, any condition which dictates to a parent in which religion he or she should bring up children interferes with that duty and, consequently, is contrary to public policy.

Public Policy and Other Conditions

It would be impossible to try to set out a list of all conditions that would be regarded as contrary to public policy. One can never really be certain whether a condition is contrary to public policy or not until it has been tested in a law court. Moreover, as society and contemporary morality change so do the questions of public policy. A judge has said: "When questions arise as to conditions or provisions being void as being against the public good or against public policy, great caution is necessary in considering them; at different times very different views have been entertained as to what is injurious to the public".

For example, let us look at a condition in a Will that a blacksmith should not carry on his trade in a certain town for six months. Now in the time of Queen Elizabeth I any condition such as this, known as a restraint of trade, was considered wrong and would have been held to be contrary to public policy. This is not the situation nowadays when a partial restraint of trade is perfectly lawful and would not be considered as contrary to public policy.

Thus, often, we can hazard only a guess at what is contrary to public policy in modern times.

Public Service

Just before the Second World War Mr. E. died and left his property to his two sons. He wanted his sons to apply themselves to his business and so, in his Will, he had inserted a condition that they should receive nothing if they were to undertake any public office prior to 1943. The Will stated "I expressly stipulate that they shall not prior to the year 1943 become candidates for or enter Parliament or undertake any other public office". His two sons wanted to join the Territorial Army and the court decided that a Territorial Army commission was a "public office". It also decided that any restraint on joining the forces was contrary to public policy and, therefore, invalid. Although this was not specifically decided, such a condition was probably void for uncertainty anyway, since "public office" is such a vague term and is open to so many interpretations. It should be remembered that this case was decided in 1939 at the beginning of the Second World War, when restrictions on joining the armed forces were viewed far more critically than they might be now.

Nevertheless, it seems that any restraint on joining the armed forced will be against public policy, and it is certainly in line with another decision which was in 1908. In that case the person making the Will left his Staffordshire estates to his nephew Herbert "provided that he does not enter into the naval or military services of the country". If Herbert should go into the naval or military services then the Staffordshire estates should go to another nephew, Francis. Such a condition was held to be contrary to public policy. "In my opinion" the judge said, "there can be few, if any, provisions more against the public good and the welfare of the state than one tending to deter persons from entering the naval or military services of the country". No doubt, had an Air Force existed such comments would have been equally applicable to that service.

A gift to someone when that person leaves the army, however, is not regarded as an inducement to leave the army but merely as provision for that person when he would need most help. Consequently, it is not contrary to public policy.

Behaviour

There have been many conditions in Wills which set conditions of behaviour upon those people who receive gifts under the Will and these usually have been upheld as enforceable. Likewise, a gift is valid if it is on condition that the person should obey the wishes of someone else, or should do something to the satisfaction of the executors.

Residence

There is nothing wrong in a condition in a Will requiring a person to live or reside either in this or some other country or in a particular house or flat, subject to the comments earlier about the public policy and marriage and the family and children.

Unlawful Acts

A condition which induces someone to commit an unlawful act is invalid. Let us say that Mr. Bloggins dislikes his neighbour Mr. Brown and decides to induce his son to inconvenience Mr. Brown. In his Will he leaves his son £500 on condition that he parks his car in Mr. Brown's driveway for three days in every week for one year. Such a condition probably is invalid because it is inducing his son to trespass on Mr. Brown's land. Mr. Bloggins might go further: he might insert a condition that his son should have £500 if, within one year of his death, he burns down Mr. Brown's house. Such a condition is clearly invalid.

What Happens if the Condition is Void?

If the condition attached to the gift is void, as in the examples above, then one of two things happens: either

1. the gift does not take effect and it goes to someone else, as provided for in the Will or, if there is no provision in the Will for it going to someone else, it becomes part of the residuary estate, or
2. the person to whom the gift is given in the Will takes the gift without the conditions being fulfilled.

If the void condition requires something to be done before the person can receive the gift, then the person does not get it. If the void condition requires something to be done after the person has received the gift, then he gets it but does not have to fulfil the condition.

How Are Conditions Enforced?

Where a condition is valid a court can enforce its observance and, if it is not complied with, the court can take away a gift which was conditional on it being done.

12

TAX CONSIDERATIONS

In a work of this size there is no scope to go into detailed tax considerations and only an outline can be attempted.

Drafting a Will so that the least amount of money is payable in tax is, for the well-off, one of the most important points to bear in mind. Tax can be extremely complex and you would be well advised to consult a solicitor or accountant or independent financial advisor to help you over these matters if you have a substantial estate of property, shares, goods and money. Very often, people have little idea of how wealthy they are. They may be living in a house for which they paid a comparatively small sum of money many years ago and find that the present value means that, on that alone without taking into account any other assets, their estate is of a value on which Inheritance Tax will be payable.

Changing Circumstances and Changing the Will
There have been some dramatic changes in our tax laws and unless one keeps on rewriting one's Will every time there is such a change, then it is possible that when one dies the law will be completely different from when one made the Will. One way in which to ensure that a minimum of tax is payable is to update the Will at frequent intervals, hoping that it will be up-to-date as to the latest tax provisions when you die. Another easier, and probably better, way of dealing with this problem is by way of variation.

Deed of Variation
This is similar to what used to be called a "deed of family arrangement".

Within two years of the death a beneficiary (someone who is entitled to receive something from the estate under the terms of the Will) entitled to any part of the dead person's estate under the terms of the Will, or the rules of intestacy, may alter that provision by a deed in writing. For the purposes of Inheritance Tax the changed provision will be regarded as having been made by the dead person and substituted for that provison in the Will or under the rules of intestacy. In other words, tax will be payable only if it is payable on the new provision. This is still true, even if the beneficiary has actually received the property and makes a gift of it or disclaims a legacy within two years from the death. Thus, if under the terms of a Will an amount of the dead person's estate is left to a son thereby incurring an Inheritance Tax liability the son can, within two years, either make a deed of variation or actually give the amount to, say, the dead person's spouse (his mother or father), thus reducing or maybe extinguishing any tax liability (because no tax is payable on gifts to a surviving spouse: see below). The law is set out in S. 142 Inheritance Tax Act 1984 (originally published as the Capital Transfer Tax Act 1984).

In order to come within the S. 142 provision, the redirection, gift or disclaimer of the particular gift or entitlement under the Will or the rules of intestacy must:

1. Be in writing;
2. Refer specifically to the actual provision in the Will which is to be varied; and
3. Be signed by the person who is entitled under the provision in the Will etc.

The deed should be sent immediately to the Capital Taxes Office. Where a person redirects property or makes a gift of it within the two year period he must give written notice to the Capital Taxes Office within six months of doing it that he wants this provision to apply. If the effect of this is to increase the liability to Inheritance Tax, then the executors must join in this notice and can refuse to do so on the ground that they do not have sufficient assets in the estate to pay the additional tax.

Death on Active Service

No Inheritance Tax is payable on the estate of a serviceman if he/she dies on active or other warlike service from a wound, accident or disease. This also applies to members of the Royal Ulster Constabulary who die from terrorist actions in Northern Ireland.

Inheritance Tax

This was introduced by the 1986 Finance Act to replace

Capital Transfer Tax. It is a tax on a "transfer of value" which,
in terms of a dead person's estate, means transfers under the
terms of the Will or the rules of intestacy which reduce the
value of the estate. It is, essentially, a tax on *gifts* and not on
commercial transactions such as sales. The amount which
becomes liable to the tax is the amount of the estate less
general exemptions which are mentioned below. For tax
purposes, the amount of the estate is the valuation of the estate
of the dead person immediately before his/her death. The tax
is levied on transfers made by the dead person on death or
within seven years of death. Consequently, if a person dies in
1992 but has made a gift in 1987 then this gift will be added to
the value of the estate, although some relief is given (see
below). As such, Inheritance Tax is quite different from
Income Tax. Income Tax is levied, after an annual allowance
or exemption, as a percentage of income received in that tax
year above that allowance. Inheritance Tax is levied, after
general exemptions, on the valuation of an estate at death
together with the amounts of substantial gifts or transfers
within the last seven years prior to the death. The scope and
size of the exemptions and the percentage of the tax levied
may change from year to year so it is always wise to check up
to see if the current value of one's estate greatly exceeds the
exemptions.

How Much Inheritance Tax Will Be Payable?
This depends on three factors:

1. The value of the estate.
2. The value of substantial gifts made during the last seven
   years.
3. Any exemptions from Inheritance Tax on one's death
   such as those on gifts to a surviving spouse, charities,
   political parties, etc.

How can I Ensure that Inheritance Tax is the Least Possible?
It is beyond the scope of this book to give complicated
financial advice and it makes no pretence to do so. Where
one's affairs are complex and there is a large estate, it is
prudent to consult a solicitor or an accountant or an
independent financial advisor. All that can be done here is to
set out some considerations when writing a Will.

If a person is domiciled in the United Kingdom the tax

applies to all that person's property wherever it may be situated at home or abroad. If the person is domiciled abroad, the tax generally applies only to property which is in the United Kingdom.

Rate of Inheritance Tax

For 1992/3 this was 40% on all the estate after exempt transfers and after the current tax threshold of £150,000. This amount is increased from 6th April each year in line with the increase in the Retail Price Index for the year to the previous December unless Parliament decides otherwise.

General Exemptions

The following are exempt for the purposes of Inheritance Tax liability.

1. All gifts between the dead person and his/her husband/ wife. If the dead person is domiciled in the United Kingdom but the husband/wife is not, then the exemption is limited to £55,000.

2. Lifetime gifts which represent normal expenditure out of the dead person's income during his/her life. Where payments are made by the dead person which did not change the dead person's standard of living then such amounts if paid during the seven years prior to the death will not be included in the estate.

3. Lifetime gifts not exceeding £3,000 in any tax year. This means that a person can make gifts totalling not more than £3,000 in any year irrespective of the number of people to whom various amounts are given, otherwise any amounts over this will be included in the value of the estate if the person dies within seven years.

4. Gifts in any one tax year to a maximum of £250 per person. There is no limit on the number of people to whom such gifts can be given so long as each one does not exceed £250 in one tax year. These amounts are additional to the £3,000 in paragraph 3 above but only to the extent that the total to any one individual in any tax year does not exceed £250. You could give £3,000 to one person and amounts of £250 to one or more people but not £3,250 to one person.

5. Gifts in consideration of marriage. Wedding gifts by a parent to his/her child are exempt up to £5,000, by a grandparent or remoter ancestor or one of the parties to the

marriage to the other up to £2,500 and by other people up to £1,000. This applies to each parent or grandparent. The gift must be to the bride or bridegroom and the wedding must take place.

6. Lifetime gifts for the maintenance of a spouse or former spouse, children and dependent relatives. In respect of a child, the exemption is until the age of 18 or completion of full-time education if later. This is available also for stepchildren and adopted children as well as for illegitimate children. The child must be of either the donor or his/her spouse.

As regards the dependent relative, the gift is exempt to the extent that it makes reasonable provision for their care or maintenance. Dependent relative means someone who is unable to maintain themselves through old age or infirmity and includes the donor's mother or mother-in-law irrespective of whether she is elderly or infirm unless she is living with her husband. So widowed mothers or mothers-in-law are included.

7. All gifts to charities.

8. Gifts to political parties unless they are made within the year of the date of death, in which case up to £100,000 is exempt but any amount above that will be included in the value of the estate.

9. Gifts to various bodies which deal with the preservation of the national heritage or of a public nature such as the National Gallery or the British Museum. This category includes gifts to most museums and art galleries. The Capital Taxes Office or a solicitor can advise.

10. Certain types of properties enjoy exemptions and reliefs. These include agricultural land, business property, historic houses, woodlands and works of art, as below.

Relief for Business Property
Since 1992 there has been 100% relief for the following categories of "relevant business property":

1. Sole proprietor or partner.

2. Life tenant's business or interest in a business.

3. A holding of shares or securities which by itself or in conjunction with other holdings owned by the transferor gives control of the company (whether quoted or unquoted).

4. Unquoted shares which by themselves or in conjunction with other shares or securities owned by the transferor give control of more than 25% of the votes.

There is 50% relief (formerly 30%) for the following:

5. Shares in a company which do not qualify under 3. above and which are not quoted on a recognised stock exchange.

6. Land, buildings, plant or machinery owned by a partner or controlling shareholder and used wholly or mainly in the business of the partnership or company immediately before the transfer, provided that the partnership interest or shareholding would itself, if it were transferred, qualify for business relief or

7. Any land or building, plant or machinery which, immediately before the transfer, was used wholly or mainly for the purposes of a business carried on by the transferor, was settled property in which he or she was then beneficially entitled to an interest in possession and was transferred while the business itself was being retained.

Potentially Exempt Transfers (PETS)
The reason we have looked so carefully at the exemptions during a person's lifetime is because any gift outside these exemptions which is made within seven years of the person's death will be included in the value of the estate. Any gift, of whatever size, and to whomsoever, which is made more than seven years from the death of the person making it is completely free from tax. These gifts are known as Potentially Exempt Transfers (PETS) and become wholly exempt once seven years have elapsed and the donor is still alive. If, however, the donor dies *within* seven years of making the gift only a percentage of the full Inheritance Tax may be payable on it, depending on how long before the death it was made, in accordance with the following scale:

If the gift is made between

6 and 7 years of the death 20% of the full tax
5 and 6 years of the death 40% of the full tax
4 and 5 years of the death 60% of the full tax
3 and 4 years of the death 80% of the full tax
death and 3 years of the death 100% of the full tax.

Gifts to a Surviving Spouse
As we have seen, any gift, whether made during life or on death, to a husband/wife is wholly exempt from Inheritance

Tax so long as he/she is domiciled in the United Kingdom.

The point to remember, however, is that when that spouse dies (which, sometimes, may not be very long after the death of his/her husband/wife) there will be no surviving spouse exemption as there will be no surviving spouse!

Much will depend on the respective ages of the spouses. It is generally accepted that women live longer than men so that if a husband leaves everything to his wife then no Inheritance Tax will be payable on his death, but in so far as the wife receives everything this will boost her estate so that, on her death, a far greater amount of Inheritance Tax may be payable. It must be remembered, however, that this may be mitigated by the annual increase in the threshold.

Life Insurance Policies

If a person takes out a policy on his/her own life and for his/her own benefit then the value of the policy forms part of his/her estate on death. If there is a gift of the policy during the person's lifetime then the premium payment, not the value of the policy, becomes a PET which will not be included in that person's estate if he/she survives for seven years after the gift. If a policy is taken out for the benefit of another person it is the premium payment, again, which is the PET and not the value of the policy. The value of the policy is normally its open market value.

Such policies can be a useful way of making provision for payment of any Inheritance Tax liability on the estate as a whole. If the policy is taken out for the benefit of another person, say a son or daughter who may be executor of the estate, then on the death of the person taking out the policy on his/her life the full maturity amount will be payable. This sum of money will be outside the estate but could be used to pay any Inheritance Tax liability, perhaps avoiding an otherwise necessary sale of house or land to pay the tax.

Moreover, very often on a person's death there is not much cash available in the estate as most of the assets may be in the house, land or stocks and shares. This can mean a rough time for, say, a surviving spouse who may have to take on the payment of a mortgage and other household outgoings. Consequently, a husband can help a wife in this difficult time by taking out a policy on his own life for her benefit which will give her the cash, outside his estate, on his death. This can also be done for a son or daughter, who will not benefit anyway from spouse exemption if any of the estate passed to them from their father and the estate was liable for Inheritance Tax.

Gifts with Reservation

One way in which a person may seek to minimise Inheritance Tax liability on death is to reduce the value of the estate by making gifts before death. We have seen already how these will be regarded as PETS and may be brought into the estate if death occurs within seven years. There is also a further pitfall. If a person gives something away but still continues to enjoy it or derives a benefit from it, then such a gift will form part of the estate whenever it was made so long as the donor continued to enjoy it, or derive a benefit from it, up to his/her death. This is known as a "gift with reservation" because the donor "reserves" a benefit. The classic case is where a widowed mother transfers into the name of her son the house in which she lives, but continues to live in it herself. If she dies still living in it, then the value of the house will be included in her estate as she has continued to derive a benefit from it. If ever she were to leave the house permanently, say, to go into a nursing home, then from that moment (not the earlier date of transfer of the house) it would become a PET and she would need to survive for a further seven years in order for the value of the house not to be included in her estate.

The point to remember is that to avoid the "gift with reservation" provision the property must be enjoyed by the person to whom it is given to the entire exclusion, or virtually to the entire exclusion, of the person giving it.

Gifts in the Will: Who Should Pay Inheritance Tax?

Whenever you leave a legacy of money to someone in your Will you should bear in mind whether you want any Inheritance Tax attributable to it to be paid out of the residue of the estate (thereby reducing the amount available for the person who receives the residue) or to be paid by the person receiving the legacy. If it is to come from the residue then the gift should be expressed to be "free of tax", whereas if it is to be paid by the person receiving the legacy then it should be expressed to be "subject to tax".

Deductions from the Estate

From the value of an estate for Inheritance Tax purposes one can deduct reasonable funeral expenses. In addition, one can deduct any additional expenses incurred in administering or realising property outside the United Kingdom against its value up to a maximum of 50% of its value.

Gifts to Charities
These are exempt at any time, whether as lifetime gifts or passing on death under the terms of the Will. They can be expressed as either to a specific charity, such as:

> "I bequeath the sum of £10,000 to the National Children's Home of 85 Highbury Park, London, N5 1UD."

or as an amount to be distributed by the dead person's trustees. These can be the same as the executors, in which case they should be named as trustees as well as executors, so that the early part of the Will would read, "I appoint my wife Ann Belinda Bloggins and my son Charles Alan Bloggins (hereinafter called my trustees) to be the executors and trustees of this my Will." The provision in the Will would then read, "I bequeath to my trustees the sum of £10,000 upon trust to be distributed to such charities as they in their absolute discretion may select, bearing in mind my wishes to benefit organisations involved in child welfare." As you can see, the dead person can suggest the kind of charity he/she wishes to benefit without specifying one or more charities by name. (See Chapter 2: Who can Benefit from a Will? page 16.)

In many cases a person makes a Will many years before his/her death. This can mean that unless the Will is revised regularly, the amounts of money specified as bequests may become devalued through inflation so that on death they do not represent the size of the gift the dead person intended. One way to overcome this is to express the gift as a percentage or proportion of the overall net estate. Thus, the provision would read, "I bequeath 10% of my net estate to the National Children's Home of 85 Highbury Park, London, N5 1UD."

If you wish your bequest to go to a particular branch of your chosen charity you must specify this in your Will, otherwise the bequest automatically goes to the charity's head office. It may give the charity greater flexibility in using your legacy if you do not refer to a specific branch, but it is worth remembering this point if you have supported a local branch for years and you especially want that branch to benefit from your Will.

In all these cases, it is always best to put the full name and address of the charity so as to minimise any confusion that might arise where different charities have similar names. These details can be obtained from the charity itself. Gifts to charities are exempt from Inheritance Tax.

Who is Liable to pay Inheritance Tax?
If a person dies within seven years of making a gift then it will be included in the estate with either the full rate of tax payable on it or only a percentage of it, depending on how many years before the death the gift is made. The scale is given elsewhere but the tax is only tapered if the gift was made more than three years before death. Within that three years, tax on the gift is at the full amount. The person primarily liable for paying the tax on such a gift is the person to whom it was given, the transferee. If however, this has not been paid to the Inland Revenue within twelve months of the death then the dead person's personal representatives (usually the executors) also become liable. This is also true where there has been a gift with reservation where the reservation is still existing at the date of death.

On all transfers made under the Will, such as legacies and bequests, the executors/administrators are liable for the payment of any Inheritance Tax due to the Inland Revenue. This is also true of transfers on intestacy. Where no specific provision for the payment of the tax has been made in the Will, then the tax is payable out of the residue, even if it means that property has to be sold in order to meet it.

Payment of Inheritance Tax by Instalments
Inheritance Tax on certain types of property may be paid by instalments rather than in one lump sum. This is obviously helpful as it means that some property which might otherwise have to be sold to pay Inheritance Tax can remain intact. The property on which tax can be paid by instalments are land and buildings, shares and securities which are unquoted on any stock exchange and hardship would result in having to pay the tax in a lump sum. You should check the rules with the Capital Taxes Office, a solicitor or accountant. You have

to give written notice to the Capital Taxes Office of a desire to pay by instalments. These then will be payable by ten equal annual amounts. In general, interest is payable on instalments.

13

SCOTLAND

The law relating to Wills in Scotland is, in many respects, similar to that in England and Wales which is contained in the rest of this book. You might find it helpful to discuss your Will with a solicitor who understands Scots law.

The more fundamental differences between Scots and English law are set out below.

Who can Make a Will?
In Scotland a boy over the age of fourteen and a girl over the age of twelve can make a Will.

The Form of the Will
In Scotland a Will is valid if it is written entirely in the handwriting of the person making the Will and signed by him. Where this is the case there is no need for the person's signature to be witnessed. The reasoning behind this is that the Will can be identified as being that of the person making it because it is in his handwriting and, therefore, there is no need for his signature to be witnessed. The whole Will must be in handwriting and not just part of it.

Whether it is handwritten or not, each page of the Will must be signed at the bottom by the person making the Will. There is no need for the witnesses to sign at the bottom of each page so long as they sign at the end of the Will.

The witnesses must write their full names, addresses and occupations at the end of the Will after the clause stating that they witnessed the signature of the person making the Will and they signed in each other's presence.

Property
If you have property in Scotland as well as in England there is no need to appoint separate trustees to deal with the property. In fact, the same trustees can deal with property in the United Kingdom and Eire.

Children
We have seen that in England and Wales the description "children" can include illegitimate and adopted children in certain circumstances. The situation in Scotland is different and you should specifically mention illegitimate and adopted children if you wish to include them in your Will.

Claims After Your Death
As we have seen, in England and Wales a person who was being maintained by you or was dependent on you during your lifetime can make a claim for money against your estate after your death, even if that person is not provided for in your Will and it is your wish that he/she should receive nothing.

In Scotland these provisions do not apply. Instead, in Scotland, there are strict legal rights that can be claimed by a widow or widower or children. These rights cannot be excluded by your Will.

On the death of a husband (or wife) if there are no children the widow (or widower) is entitled to claim half of all the estate's moveable assets, which really means all things such as personal effects, furniture and cars, but not land or houses or flats. If there are children then the widow or widower can claim one third of the moveable assets which includes cash and securities for cash. Children have the right to claim one half of the moveable assets of their mother or father who has just died if their other parent is already dead. They can claim one third of the moveable assets if the other parent is still alive. The widow or widower and children have to decide whether they wish to claim their legal rights, as set out above, or whether they wish to take property left to them in the Will according to the terms of the Will. They cannot have it both ways.

You can see from these rules that it is very difficult to disinherit your wife/husband and children because, after your death, they will be able to claim their legal rights. The point to note, however, is that these claims are against moveable assets only. So if you were to sell most of your moveable goods and spend your money on buying land and houses then there would be very little against which to claim.

Revocation

We have seen that in England and Wales if a person marries after making a Will then the Will becomes inoperative or, in other words, the Will is revoked by the marriage unless the Will was made in contemplation of marriage. In Scotland if a person marries after making a Will that does not revoke it. In Scotland, however, if you make a Will without mentioning any children not yet born and a child is in fact born after the Will has been made, then that will have the effect of the Will being presumed to have been revoked.

Consequently, if you make no provision for any future children and a child is born after you have made your Will then you should make a new Will.

Intestacy

In Scotland the law is different from that in England and Wales if you die without leaving a Will (see Chapter 8, page 108).

1. If there is a surviving spouse only and no children or other descendants, no parents, brothers, sisters or their children then the surviving spouse takes the whole estate.
2. If there is a surviving spouse and children, the surviving spouse takes the house (or £50,000 if it is worth more than that), furniture and personal belongings up to £10,000, any cash up to £15,000, and one third of the remaining moveable estate. The rest is divided equally among the children, or any of their children if they have died. You should remember that any money given to a child by the person who has died during his lifetime will be taken off the amount the child receives.
3. If there is no surviving spouse but children are alive, then the estate is divided equally among the children which includes illegitimate and adopted but not step-children. If any have died, then their share is divided up among their own children.
4. If there is no surviving spouse nor children but parents, brothers and sisters who are alive, then half the estate is

taken by the parents equally and half goes equally to all
the brothers and sisters, or their children if any of them
have died. If only one of these groups is available then
the whole estate goes to that particular group. Half
brothers and half sisters will only be entitled if there are
no full brothers or full sisters.

5. If there is no surviving spouse and no close relatives then
   the estate is distributed to the following groups, in that
   order:

   full uncles and aunts or their children
   half uncles and aunts or their children
   grandparents
   full great uncles and aunts or their descendants
   half great uncles and aunts or their descendants
   great grandparents.

If there are no relatives who can be found, then the whole
estate is taken by the Crown which may make gifts to people
who may make a claim if they were closely involved with the
deceased.

14

SERVICEMEN

The special position of servicemen was recognised as early as
1677 when, under the Statute of Frauds, S. 22 "Provided
alwayes that notwithstanding this Act any soldier being in
actuall Military service or any marriner or seaman being at sea
may dispose of his moveables, wages and personall estate as he
or they might have done before the makeing of this Act".

This was re-enacted by S. 11 of the Wills Act 1837, which is
the basis of the law relating to Wills.

There was some ambiguity which was resolved by The Wills
(Soldiers and Sailors) Act, 1918, which declared that a minor
in actual military service or who is a mariner or seaman at sea
can make a Will. Moreover, this extends to any member of
naval or marine forces not only when he is at sea, but also
when he is in circumstances which, if he were a soldier, would
be regarded as being in actual military service. "Soldier"

includes a member of the Royal Air Force and, under these provisions a serviceman can deal in his Will not only with personal property but also with land.

The term "actual military service" means "active military service" and any soldier, sailor or airman is entitled to make a serviceman's Will if he is actually serving with the armed forces in connection with operations which are or have been taking place or are believed to be imminent. This means that the serviceman must be directly concerned with operations in a war which is or has been in progress or is imminent. Thus, it does not apply to a soldier in B.A.O.R. during peacetime but it did apply to a soldier under orders to go to the Falklands when that country was invaded by Argentina.

It has now been firmly established that a soldier serving with the Security Forces in Northern Ireland is in "actual military service" for the purpose of S.11 of the Wills Act, 1837.

A Will by a serviceman may be made either in writing or by word of mouth. There is no need to prove that he knew he was making a Will or that he was entitled to. It is sufficient if the serviceman intends to state what he wants done with his possessions on his death.

Thus, 2/Lt.S.Royal Warwickshire Regt., on 6th July, 1917, was on orders to leave for France. On that day he said to Miss D. "If I stop a bullet everything of mine will be yours". He was killed in action on 9th October, 1917. It was held by the court that this was a valid soldier's Will and Miss D. was entitled to his property.

If a serviceman's Will is in writing it may be written in pencil, have only one witness or no witness at all.

The important point is that the serviceman, mariner or seaman must intend his words to be acted upon as being an effective Will. It is not enough for him merely to inform someone else about his affairs without an intention that his words should be remembered and should be acted on by the person to whom they were spoken.

The usual rule about people who witness a Will is that they cannot be given a gift in that Will. This rule, however, does not apply to servicemen's Wills and any person witnessing a serviceman's Will can also be a beneficiary, that is, receive something from the Will.

The only exception to the informality of a serviceman's Will is when the Will is dealing with wages payable by the

Admiralty or to merchant seamen by the Board of Trade. There are special rules relating to this.

Revoking a Serviceman's Will

A serviceman can *revoke* a previous Will whether made formally or informally by an informal declaration. He cannot do this if he returns to civilian life: there is then the need for a formal revocation which we have already dealt with.

A serviceman who is still a minor when he returns to civilian life cannot revoke a previous Will at all until he reaches the age of eighteen.

Should a Serviceman Make a Formal Will?

Notwithstanding these provisions enabling a serviceman to make an informal Will these can lead to problems. It is advisable, therefore, for a serviceman to make a formal Will just like anyone else.

Death on Active Service

No tax is payable on the estate (see Chapter 12: Tax Considerations, page 131).

Seamen

Where a seaman dies whilst serving or within six months of serving in certain circumstances the Board of Trade is empowered to deal with any of his property either on the ship or in any country outside the U.K. The Board of Trade can distribute such property between the next-of-kin, the seaman's widow or child (including both adopted and illegitimate), any persons entitled to the property under the seaman's Will and any creditors.

15

HOW PROBATE IS OBTAINED

This chapter is a brief guide to what is involved in obtaining probate so that the estate of a dead person can be administered. The actual document which is issued by the Probate Registry is known as a grant of representation.

If the estate is worth a large amount of money or if it is complicated by settled property to which the dead person was entitled, then the executor should consult a solicitor to obtain probate. Moreover, he should see a solicitor if there is a problem about tracing persons who are to receive something under the Will, or if the dead person did not leave a Will and there are relatives of whose whereabouts he is not sure.

The executor is empowered to deal with the dead person's estate as from the date of death. Grant of probate merely confirms his powers through the document called the grant of representation and is proof to the world. Where there is no Will, or where there is a Will but no executor named in it, then Letters of Administration have to be obtained. This is also the case where the executors cannot apply or do not wish to. The procedure is similar to that for obtaining probate and is dealt with below.

Is Probate Necessary?

It is not always necessary to obtain probate where the amounts in the estate are small and, in such circumstances, an executor or personal representative can obtain these amounts without making an application for probate at all. This applies mainly to assets held by bodies such as the Department for National Savings, building societies, etc. None of these bodies is legally obliged to make payment without seeing probate or Letters of Administration and if there are any complications they will probably insist on it. Nevertheless, most will be helpful and make payment if the amounts are small. Even banks or insurance companies may pay over small amounts in straightforward cases without insisting on a grant of probate. In the case of National Savings or premium bonds, you can obtain from a Post Office a form (SB4), which is simple to fill in, and a prepaid envelope. A grant of probate is almost certain to be required in the case of company shares or stock, whether the holding is small or large.

You will need a grant of probate or Letters of Administration to transfer or sell any property which was in the sole name of the dead person, but where a property is in joint names a grant is usually unnecessary as the survivor takes over the whole property by operation of law. If you need to sell a house do not put it on the market before you have obtained the grant.

Where There is a Will

A sole executor appointed by the Will will obtain probate. If there are two or several executors, then it is not necessary for all to obtain probate: the application can be made by any of the executors up to a maximum of four.

Where There is a Will but no Executors Named

The person entitled to apply for a grant of probate or Letters of Administration is the one who is named in the Will as being entitled to all the estate, or all the residue of the estate, after specific gifts and bequests have been made. This also applies where there are executors named in the Will but they cannot or do not wish to apply for a grant of probate or Letters of Administration.

Where There is no Will

In this case, application should be made by the next-of-kin of the dead person. This will be:

1. the widow (widower) or, if none,
2. a child of the dead person, or, if none,
3. a parent of the dead person or, if none,
4. a brother or sister of the dead person or, if none,
5. other relatives.

If any children or brothers or sisters of the dead person who would have been entitled to apply according to the list above have died during the lifetime of the dead person, then their children may apply instead.

In order to apply, the person must be over the age of 18. So if the dead person left no spouse but a child aged 17 and a brother aged 40 then it is the brother who should apply. Children includes illegitimate children but other illegitimate relatives may not be entitled to a grant. A Probate Registry Office will help on this if someone is uncertain. It may be possible for someone to apply on behalf of someone else but, again, a Registry or Office will advise.

Where is the Application Made?

Application can be made to the nearest, or most convenient, local Probate Registry or Probate Office, to be found in the telephone directory. They will provide a list of addresses of local Probate Registries and Offices, of which there is one in most major towns. You should never write to a Probate *Office*, only to the Probate *Registry* which controls that particular office. All correspondence should be addressed to the Personal Application Section at the relevant Registry.

Alternatively, you can write or telephone the London Personal Application Department:

> Probate Personal Application Department
> 2nd Floor
> Somerset House
> Strand
> London
> WC2R 1LP
> Telephone: 071 936 6983

When making a personal application to a probate *Office* the executor or personal representative of the dead person should check the time that it is open. When you receive the forms from the Probate Registry there should be included a list of the local Offices giving their opening days and times.

What Has to be Done?

The next-of-kin should register the death with the registrar of births and deaths whose address he can find in the telephone directory. This will enable him to obtain a *death certificate* and copies of the death certificate for inclusion in letters that he, or the executor, if different, will have to write.

He should then obtain the dead person's *Will*. Hopefully, he will know where this is to be found, whether at home or deposited in the bank, because the dead person should have told him during his/her lifetime where it was placed. If the next-of-kin is also the executor, or one of the executors, named in the Will then it is likely that he will know where the Will has been kept. The executor should then take a photocopy of the Will and keep it with him, just in case the original one is later lost.

He will need to obtain *full details* of the dead person's estate. He should draw up a list of the property such as house, flat, land, cash, stocks and shares, bank account, savings, and including property and amounts that were due on death such as insurance policies. The executor should also have details of personal property such as car, jewellery, furniture, clothes, etc.

He will have to obtain a valuation of these items. On many of the items he can estimate this himself, trying to make them as accurate as possible.

In the case of the *bank account* he should write to the Bank Manager stating that he is the executor of the dead person, giving the full name and date of death. He should ask the Bank Manager to let him know the amount of money in the dead person's accounts together with any other details that might be helpful, such as any securities or valuables that were deposited at the bank. Moreover, the Bank Manager may be able to tell him the names of any companies in which the dead person had stocks and shares.

If he has the share certificates, he will be able to write to the Bank Manager giving details of the stocks and shares and asking him to find out their valuation on the date of death.

If the case of an *insurance policy* he should write to the insurance company stating that he is the executor of the dead person, giving the full name and date of death, and asking what amount is payable under the policy.

In the case of *National Savings Certificates* he should write to the Savings Certificate Office, Durham, and ask for a list of all certificates that were held by the dead person, their date of purchase and their value at the date of death. As with the Bank Manager and insurance company he should state that he is the executor of the dead person, giving the full name and the date of death.

In the case of *premium bonds* he should write to the Bond and Stock Office, Lytham St. Annes, Lancashire, giving the full name and date of death. Premium bonds remain in the draw for 12 months from death, so they can be left invested for that time, or, if preferred, encashed when probate has been obtained. Form SB4 (obtainable from Post Offices) is used to notify death and obtain repayment of many Government savings instruments.

In the case of the *house* or *flat* the executor needs to put a value on it. This can be his assessment or that of a professional valuer but it is always subject to the Inland Revenue asking their District Valuer to determine the value if they cannot agree it with the executor. If there is a mortgage, the executor should write to the mortgagee (the building society or bank or local authority as the case may be) stating the same information as to the Bank Manager and insurance company and asking for the amount outstanding on the date of death.

If there is any pension fund or other money to which the dead person is entitled then the executor should write to the employers or institutions, stating the same information as to the Bank Manager and asking for full details.

Moreover, he should list any money that was owed to the dead person, which he/she should have received had he/she not died.

He should now make a list of all the *debts* that the dead person owed because these will have to be paid out of the estate. These are not just loans that the dead person might have received during his/her lifetime but include all bills, overdrafts, hire purchase liabilities, rates, etc. If there is any doubt about the extent of the debts then the executor can advertise in the London Gazette and a newspaper which circulates in the area in which the estate is situated, although, in addition, he must do all he can to bring the dead person's death to the attention of any possible creditors about whose existence he may be aware. The advertisement advises creditors that they must submit claims by a certain date, (at least two months away) after which the executor can distribute the estate having obtained probate.

One debt for which the estate may be liable and about which the executor may have no knowledge is if the dead person gave a guarantee to another person during his lifetime. Hopefully, if this is the case, the person making the Will would have foreseen the difficulty for his executor and will have left a clear note with the Will to the effect that he did give a guarantee. If not, then this is something that the executor must bear in mind as a possible claim on the estate.

Once the funeral has taken place he should ask the funeral directors for their account so as to know the exact amount of the *funeral expenses*.

Finally, the executor should write to the local Inspector of Taxes to see if there is any income tax liability of the dead person or whether the estate is entitled to any tax refund.

How is the Application Made?

The executor will need to obtain the application form, decide where he wishes to be interviewed, send the completed forms together with the *death certificate* and the original (not the photocopy) *Will* to the appropriate Probate Registry and then go for the interview. He can obtain the forms from the local Probate Registry or Probate Office as described in "Where the Application is Made" above. These will consist of the following:

1. a blue and white one, form PR83
2. a blue one, Cap 44
3. a yellow one, Cap 37
4. a yellow one, Cap 40
5. a large brown pre-addressed envelope, for returning the forms
6. a booklet entitled "How to Obtain Probate", form PR 48.

Filling in the Forms

FORM PR 83: Probate Application Form
The executor has to complete the name of the Probate Registry or local Office where he wishes to be interviewed and the full name, address, occupation, age, marital status and dates of birth and death of the dead person. He has to complete details of the Will, of relatives of the dead person, and of himself. He must also give the names of any other executors and their details if they are applying as well. If they are not applying, he must state the reason why not as one of the following:

A   died before the deceased
B   died after the deceased
C   does not wish to apply
D   does not wish to apply now but may later.

FORM Cap 44: A Return of the Whole Estate
The executor must not be frightened by the size of this form which has eight numbered pages to fill in. It is self-explanatory and not difficult to complete if read carefully. If he has any problems or worries about some of the questions, then he must ask about them. The form asks for details of the dead person's estate and the executor should sign the declaration at the bottom of the last page.

FORM Cap 37: Inland Revenue Capital Taxes Office
This recently-introduced form is concerned with Inheritance Tax and replaces the previous Cap 37 form which referred to

the old Capital Transfer Tax. It requires details of any real, leasehold, heritable and immovable property (e.g. land, house, flats on a long lease) which belonged to the dead person whose name and date of death should be entered at the top. The executor must also fill in his own name and address. All the land and buildings which form part of the dead person's estate should be listed. In column 2 he should put the description, e.g. "1, Whiteacre, Blacktown, in the County of Greenshire". In column 3 he should enter whether it is "freehold" or "leasehold". In column 4 he should enter any tenancies of the land or buildings. In column 5 he should enter any agricultural part: this is for certain relief from taxation. In column 6 he should enter the value: either his own estimate, that of an estate agent or surveyor or that of the District Valuer.

Where land or buildings belonging to the dead person's estate are sold by the executor or person who inherits them within three years from the date of death at a lower price than the valuation as at the date of death, then the Inland Revenue will allow that lower price to be substituted for the purposes of assessing any Inheritance Tax payable.

FORM Cap 40: Inland Revenue Capital Taxes Office
This is a form for listing all stocks and shares and securities which are held by the dead person as at the date of death.

The rules on valuation for the purpose of Inheritance Tax are explained clearly in a booklet which can be obtained free of charge from

> The Capital Taxes Office
> Minford House
> Rockley Road
> London W14 0DF (tel: 071 603 4622).

The Stock Market Crash of 19th October 1987 left everyone in no doubt that share prices can change dramatically in a very short space of time. Obviously, if the value of shares which were valued as at the date of death suddenly plummet shortly afterwards, then those who are due to inherit them will be left with a much smaller value. Moreover, Inheritance Tax liability would be based on the valuation at the date of death giving a much higher liability. The Inland Revenue are sympathetic to such a situation and there is provision whereby if the executor or the person who inherits the shares sells them within twelve months of death they may claim that the total of the sale prices (before deduction of any expenses such as stockbrokers' commission) should be substituted for the death value. This provision, however, applies to *all* the shares sold within twelve months of the death, not just to those which have fallen in value. Consequently, if the executor or person inheriting the shares wishes to gain the benefit of this provision, then he should sell within twelve months of the death only those shares which have fallen in value and wait until after the twelve months to sell those which have not fallen or have actually increased in value.

Sending off the Forms
The executor should make sure that he sends or delivers the following documents:

1. Completed forms PR 83, Cap 44, Cap 37, Cap 40
2. The death certificate
3. The Will (keeping a copy in case the original is lost in the post).

If there is no Will but there is a letter or other document in which the dead person expressed his/her wishes about the way in which his/her estate is to be distributed, then this should be included.

Even though the executor will have set out in Section 1 of form PR 83 where he wishes to be interviewed, if there are any dates or times which are inconvenient then these should be included in a covering letter. The interview, of which there must be at least one before grant of probate or Letters of Administration can be issued, must take place during working hours of the Probate Registry or local Office.

The forms must be sent to the Probate Registry at which the interview is to take place or the Probate Registry which controls the local Office at which the interview is to take place. They must not be sent to a local office. If the forms are being *sent* rather than *delivered* it is preferable to do so by recorded delivery or registered post. It may be possible for the interview to take place on the same day as the forms are delivered to the appropriate Probate Registry or local office. The forms can be *delivered* personally to either a Probate Registry or local office.

The Appointment at the Probate Registry/Office
The people in the Probate Registries and local offices are used
to dealing with personal applications by ordinary people so
there need be no fear of going to ask questions. The staff are
both sympathetic and helpful and the atmosphere is informal.

The appointment is to iron out problems and to get the
executor to swear or affirm before the Probate Officer that the
information in the forms is true to the best of his knowledge.
The taxation form for Inheritance Tax purposes has to be
signed so that this can be submitted to the Capital Taxes Office
for the assessment to be made of any Inheritance Tax payable.
If the net estate (after exempt bequests) is below the threshold,
then no tax is payable (see Chapter 12: Tax Considerations,
page 132). There can be no grant of probate or Letters of
Administration until any Inheritance Tax payable (or the first
instalment of it) has been paid.

At the interview the executor will be asked to pay the
probate fees which are worked out on the value of the net
estate. He should arrive at the interview with a cheque for the
amount payable of which an estimate will have been sent
beforehand if possible. These fees may amount to several
hundreds of pounds in the case of larger estates. A list of
current fees, the amount of which increase with size of the net
estate, can be obtained from the Probate Registry or local
office to give an indication of what will be payable.

Although generally only one interview is necessary there
may have to be a subsequent one if the estate is complicated
and other documents have to be signed or other people have to
be contacted. These might include any witnesses to the Will
where it is necessary to clarify any matter.

After the interview the Probate Registry will send the
account of the estate to the Capital Taxes Office for an
assessment of any Inheritance Tax payable. On very many
estates no tax is payable at all. Once the Probate Registry has
received notification from the Capital Taxes Office, this will be
sent to the executor who will have been told about the
arrangements for payment at the interview.

Payment of Inheritance Tax
In general this must be paid before probate or Letters of
Administration can be granted. It must be paid within six
months of the date of death but actually on delivery of the

account to the Probate Registry if this takes place before the end of the six month period. Tax on Potentially Exempt Transfers which becomes chargeable is due six months after the end of the month in which the death occurs. There are situations in which tax can be paid in instalments as explained on page 139.

If it is intended to pay tax by instalments then written notice must be given to the Capital Taxes Office.

Where there is a personal application for grant of probate or Letters of Administration the Probate Registry will inform the executor or personal representative how much tax must be paid before the grant can be obtained and the address at which the tax should be paid. It is possible for certain National Savings held by the dead person to be transferred directly to the Inland Revenue in payment of tax and certain property can be handed over as well. This includes land and buildings which are of historic interest and their contents and pictures, prints, books, manuscripts, works of art, scientific objects or other items which are approved as being of similar interest.

Grant of Probate/Letters of Administration

After a few weeks the executor will receive the grant. This is a single sheet of paper which sets out that the dead person of his address died on the particular day and that the executor, who is named with his address, has been granted the administration of the estate. It also sets out the gross and net value of the estate and is dated. Attached to it is the probate copy of the Will. The executor will receive back the original death certificate. It should be remembered that the grant of probate/Letters of Administration and the Will become public property in that they are open to inspection by members of the public.

Upon payment of a modest fee per copy, the executor can obtain from the Probate Registry further sealed office copies of the grant of probate. These are photocopies but bear the official embossed seal on them. They are particularly useful if there is a large number of organisations to contact in order to release property in the name of the dead person. For it is the grant of probate which gives the executor legal authority to deal with the dead person's property and it will need to be shown to all those organisations which require sight of it: the Bank Manager, the registrar of any company in which the dead person had shares, insurance companies, etc. In the case of shares, for example, the registrar of the company will stamp the reverse of the grant of probate or a sealed office copy to the effect that probate has been exhibited to the company and that a new share certificate can be issued in the name of the executor or the person to whom that part of the estate is to be distributed under the terms of the Will. Probate means that all these assets can be released and the executor can fully administer the estate.

APPENDIX

Wills may be deposited at:

> Principal Registry of the Family Division
> Record Keepers Department
> Room 28
> Somerset House
> Strand
> London WC2R 1LP
> (071 936 7000).

Make your cheque/postal order for the fee of £1 payable to "H.M. Paymaster General".

For Northern Ireland, contact:

> The Master of the Probate and Matrimonial Office
> The Royal Courts of Justice
> Chichester Street
> Belfast BT1 3JF
> (0232 235111 ext 2238).

The fee is also £1.

INDEX

Readers may be interested in the wide range of **Paperfronts** available. A full catalogue can be had by sending S.A.E. to the address below.

ELLIOT RIGHT WAY BOOKS, KINGSWOOD, SURREY, U.K.